S0-AAB-699

Brand Yourself for College Students

Endorsements

Your college years will be over soon. Start working on your personal brand now so that you'll be ready when you're looking for your first great job. Read this book to help you build your personal brand step-by-step.

James Malinchak
Co-Author, Chicken Soup for the College Soul
"2-Time College Speaker of the Year!"
Founder, www.BigMoneySpeaker.com

Glory Borgeson has written an important book. The truth is that this book should be required reading for those about to graduate. I recommend it highly and I'm proud of Ms. Borgeson. All that, plus it's a very delightful read.

Jay Conrad Levinson
The Father of Guerrilla Marketing
Author, Guerrilla Marketing *series of books*

I've interviewed and managed many people during my career. If the younger candidates and employees I meet can learn and apply Glory's techniques from *Brand Yourself!,* they definitely will stand out and experience more success, early-on.

Al Lautenslager
Author, Guerrilla Marketing in 30 Days

With a daughter about to graduate from college and two more children soon to follow her, I was thrilled to learn Glory had the inspiration and took the initiative to write this book. She's created a clear path for developing the needed advantage to stand out. *Brand Yourself* is the perfect gift for all college students seeking to jump-start their careers.

David Handler
The Coach, Success Handler, LLC

Just like car manufacturers brand each of their models for a particular type of customer, you need to brand yourself for a particular type of "customer" in the workplace who you want to hire you. Read this book to learn how to do it!

Cynthia Starz,
Managing Director - Human Resources
United Airlines

If ever there were a time when college students needed straight talk on how to make themselves more employable, "pickable," and career-ready, it's now. As an entrepreneur who owns a company that has a successful internship program and hires the best and brightest young talent, I can say that *Brand Yourself! for College Students: How to Use Personal Branding to Get the Job You Want!* is THE definitive guide. Too many books skirt around the issues facing college students today; this book nails them head on. It doesn't just tell students what to watch out for or condemn them; it gives real-life solutions to real-world challenges often masquerading as "stupid things." Students who read this book and put its advice into practice will be more likely to get hired by someone like me—everyone else may well be still looking for a job.

Lena L. West
Serial entrepreneur, blogger, columnist, & Social Media Strategist

What a great primer for college students who need to hear what they need to do now to get, first, the internships and, later, jobs as they pass their college milestones. Glory tells it like it is with loads of examples to guarantee that these students remember that looking for a job is a job itself. What makes this book such a great one is that she creates a sense of urgency throughout—starting with branding and creating a value proposition that lets the reader know what preparation each job seeker needs to do; and then she provides the tools with some very practical exercises to engage the reader to keep working toward the goal each person also needs to have in mind.

Matt DeLuca
HR consultant; author of Best Answers to the 201 Most Frequently
Asked Interview Questions, (New York University)*;*
Baruch College adjunct faculty member; Blogster–HR Killer Skills

I can't say strongly enough how important it is to have a personal brand! This is especially true when seeking a job. Add to this the fact that for a recent college graduate, the job market is a HUGE challenge right now and is unfortunately getting more difficult. If you don't work at making yourself stand out, the prospects of finding a job right now are bleak. Glory Borgeson has written a tremendous book, giving you the tools to establish a personal brand that will separate you from the competition. What are you waiting for? Believe me, the jobs are not going to come knocking on your door. Do yourself a favor: buy this book, read it, follow the very clear steps to building your personal brand, and go out and show the world who you are!

Stephen Harap, Ph.D.
Executive Coach and Talent Development Expert

Personal branding is not about your image. It goes well beyond a new outfit and a haircut. Your brand tells a story to others and comes from your entire self. *Brand Yourself! for College Students* is the perfect how-to manual for making sure that all of your "pieces" are working together to present who you really are to others and you move your career in the right direction.

Dave Saunders,
New Media and Communications Specialist
DaveSaunders.net

FOR

COLLEGE STUDENTS

How to Use Personal Branding to Get the Job You Want!

GLORY BORGESON

PINNACLE
PUBLICATIONS, INC.

Copyright © 2010 by Glory Borgeson. All rights reserved.

No part of this book may be reproduced, stored in a retrieval system in any form or by any means, electronic, mechanical, photocopying, recording, scanning or otherwise without permission of the Publisher. Requests to the Publisher for permission should be addressed to:

Pinnacle Publications, Inc.
P. O. Box 4224
Wheaton, IL 60189

Design: Wayne E. Johnson
wayneej@comcast.net

ISBN: 978-0-9820507-5-0

First printing 2010

Printed in the United States of America

10 9 8 7 6 5 4 3 2 1

Table of Contents

Disclaimer

This book is designed to provide information about finding a job. It is sold with the understanding that the publisher and author are not engaged in rendering legal services. If legal assistance is required, the services of a competent professional should be sought.

The purpose of this book is to educate and inform. The author and Pinnacle Publications, Inc. shall have neither liability nor responsibility to any person or entity with respect to any loss or damage caused, or alleged to have been caused, directly or indirectly, by the information contained in this book.

Acknowledgements

When I thought about taking the message of personal branding to college students, I was already writing and speaking about it for adults in the corporate and entrepreneurial world. Since I was hearing stories from hiring managers of their experiences working with employees in their 20s (and stories about interviewing college students for their post-collegiate jobs), I realized college students need to know how to brand themselves well so that they can get the job they want in their career field and then continue to get the future promotions they want. (I also realized many were not doing this well at all.)

First, I'd like to thank all of the people on college campuses who want to help students get the strategies they need to get the job they want, such as Student Activities Directors and Career Center Directors (and all of their staff members, too).

Thanks to all of the hiring managers out there who've generously shared their stories with me about working with employees between the ages of 20 and 29, as well as your interview stories with this age group. These are a treasure trove for me. Please keep them coming!

I'd like to thank three students who took time out of their busy schedules to review an early draft of this book: Gabe Rodriguez, Brad Churchman, and John Markle. References to outdated items (such as "tapes") were changed, better examples were added, explanations were made clearer, and lame humor was eliminated (hopefully) thanks to their suggestions.

To the endorsers of this book: Thank you for your support and kind words! Your testimonials are so valuable to me!

James Malinchak, Jay Conrad Levinson, Al Lautenslager, David Handler, Cynthia Starz, Lena L. West, Matt DeLuca, Stephen Harap, and Dave Saunders.

Why Should You *Brand Yourself*?

Kevin started his senior year of college with confidence. He got A's and B's in his first three years. During his junior year, he persuaded his fraternity brothers to clean up their acts so that they weren't perceived as goof-offs on campus, and then he won an election to an officer position for his senior year. He participated in various sports through campus intramurals, was fairly popular with the girls, easily took on anyone who challenged him to a video game, and figured his future was bright.

Kevin had heard from other students in classes ahead of him that the campus recruiting program for jobs after graduation was pretty good. He heard the companies that came to his school's campus were really good to work for, too. He knew about a résumé workshop offered by the Career Center and took advantage of that to write a decent résumé. Even the staff thought Kevin's subsequent résumé was great. He had a couple summer job experiences he included on it which showed he had a good work ethic. All of his bosses from previous jobs really liked him, and he planned to ask them to be references.

Kevin had a plan: *"I'll go to all of the campus recruiting events. From that, I'll get several job interviews lined up with as many of the companies as possible. I'll take the Career Center's workshop on interviewing skills. I'll get picked by two or three of the companies for a second interview. And then from those, I'll get between one and three job offers."*

When Kevin showed up for the recruiting events, he was one of hundreds of students. Just trying to get five minutes with a company representative was a challenge. At each booth, his résumés were added to a pile of other peoples' résumés. He got some of the company representatives' business cards. Kevin followed up with those people by sending e-mails. But he only got one interview out of the entire process.

After that one interview, he didn't get a callback for a second. And he didn't have any other plan in place for getting more interviews. Graduation day was looming.

In the meantime, a few of his friends who had the same major were getting more interviews, but not all as a result of their contacts from the campus recruiting events. Kevin wondered how they got those other interviews. Then he found out that one of those friends, Rob, got a job offer. So Kevin decided to ask Rob how he did it.

As it turns out, Rob had contacts outside of the school who had been in communication with him regularly since his junior year. Rob also had recently been looking the part and sounding the part of an employee, seeming more like a 27-year-old than a 21-year old, especially when he was in front of anyone older than a college student.

Kevin asked Rob what he talked about with his contacts and during his interviews. Rob only revealed a little about that, but hinted that even though he wasn't going into sales, he, in fact, had to "sell himself" as a future employee of a company. Rob also figured out how to highlight his strengths against his competition's weaknesses, and he figured out what the hiring managers wanted in a new employee.

In short, Rob figured out that he had to *create a brand* (namely, himself) and then sell it. Just like a car company creates a new model and has to figure out ways to sell the car to the public, Rob figured out how to create his *personal brand* and how to sell it to potential employers.

~ ~ ~ ~ ~ ~ ~ ~ ~ ~ ~ ~ ~ ~ ~

For any freshman just starting college, it can feel like there is a long road ahead to graduation. Four long years. Many tests, papers, and hours of studying lie ahead.

Then you blink a few times, and you're a senior. Where did the time go?

And then you have to find a *job* for after graduation (which, you prefer, is in your chosen career field).

A lot of people want the same job you want. They're all writing résumés. They'll all go for the same job interviews.

Who's going to get that job?

The hiring managers get to decide who they want to interview, and then from that group of people, they get to decide who they want to hire.

Later, they get to decide who they want to promote. (These hiring managers have all of the responsibility *and* all of the control.)

So how do you make yourself favorable in the eyes of these hiring managers?

You do it by *branding yourself.*

When you brand yourself, you will do something similar to companies that brand their products. (More about that later.)

Many people call it *personal branding.*

When you brand yourself, you work on several areas (both inside yourself and outside), and then you use that to "sell yourself" for the job.

One of the interesting things about personal branding is that most people don't bother to do it. And since they don't, **other people decide** what their "brand" is for them.

One of my mottos is: "*If you don't brand yourself, someone else will; and it probably won't be the brand you want!*"

If you don't decide what your personal brand will be and then promote it in that way, other people will decide *who you are, what your brand is*, and they will promote that instead. Most of the time, you will not like the brand that someone else chooses for you.

While you're looking for your first post collegiate job, you have the opportunity to create your personal brand and then promote it. This is your time to figure out how to outshine your competition for the job. Since you're learning about this now, you also have the chance to tweak your personal brand over time by rereading this book and making adjustments according to where life takes you and where you want your career to go. Your knowledge about personal branding will help you take your career to new places that many people never figure out before they retire.

Personal branding is very important for new graduates on several levels:

- More people are looking for jobs than there are jobs to fill. This is especially true for new graduates who prefer a job in their career field. (The supply and demand for jobs ebbs and flows with the condition of the economy. But you will almost always find with each graduating class that many do not find a job in their chosen field for a while.)
- Many of your peers are not being wise about how they present themselves to hiring managers.
- Too many people between 20 and 25 are being foolish about their online presence (which is easy for potential employers to find).
- Most hiring managers have a negative story to tell about working with people in their 20s. Their experiences often lead them to choose to hire a 35-year-old (when they would have normally hired a new graduate) so that they don't have to deal with an unknown maturity factor.
- Not only are you competing with people in your age group—if a hiring manager fits into the previous bullet point, you're also competing with people who are a little older who have more experience.

Twenty-plus years ago, when college-age people made poor choices (that resulted in being arrested or that involved some type of sophomoric stunt), a story about it might have appeared in their college newspaper. Those newspapers, however, were exclusively printed on paper. Today, those papers sit in an archive somewhere. You can't Google the former students' names and come up with those articles. (Maybe someday you will be able to when the content is placed online, but by that time those former students will be well over 40 years old. By then, their prospective employer won't really care what happened to them more than 20 years earlier.)

In more recent years, however, many colleges have placed their newspapers online. As their graduates moved on to new lives and new careers, those who had negative articles written about them, describing their arrests or goofy stunts, found that those articles are still available online (much to their chagrin).

Those Google-able graduates have been contacting their alma maters requesting the schools to take down the articles describing their poor choices *when they were college students.*

The schools are responding to their requests by stating: *No, we won't.*

Meanwhile, you would wonder why an employer would care what a prospective employee, who is now 27, did when they were 21 and in college. It's a good question–maybe some employers figure that people don't change much over time. It's not true; a lot of people change over time, even over six years. But, in this case, it's the employer's call.

So, what does this mean for you?

It means you can learn a lesson from the people who are now between 27 and 35. If you do something unwise and it winds up in your school paper (or in a town paper, blog, "online TV," etc.), the bad news may be there for a long, long time. Future potential employers will be able to find the negative article and know something about you that you don't want them to know. Even if you have a fairly common name, using your name and your school's name in a search engine, the article may still be easy to find.

The moral of this story is: *You are branding yourself now when you're not even trying. Stay out of trouble. If you don't, it may come back to haunt you later.*

One of the biggest problems your age group has is the **negative press** you've received regarding workplace behaviors. Many journalists and managers have written about what it's like to work with people between the ages of 20 and 29, and the stories aren't pretty. I have a file folder filled with articles telling these types of tales.

Most of the stories have to do with people in your age group (college graduates in their first or second job) making really immature choices in the workplace. The thing that makes the stories so shocking to people who are older than you are is 1) Very few people in the previous generation did the kinds of things we read about in those articles and 2) There is a larger percentage of people in your age group making these immature choices than in past generations.

Since so many people in your age group make immature choices in the workplace (notice I did *not* say the word *all*), the older folks tend to put you all in the same boat and *brand all of you as being immature.*

You might be thinking, "*That's not fair. I'm not like that. I don't act like that.*"

You're probably thinking the truth. In fact, just because some people in their 20s make poor choices in the workplace doesn't mean you will, too. Unfortunately, the burden is on you to prove it. Fortunately, you can do that by *branding yourself,* and by doing it well.

When you *brand yourself,* you will do something similar to companies that brand their products.

Nike does it.
Coca-Cola does it.
BMW does it.
Hershey's does it.

They all have products they want you to buy. And that's not all–they want you to feel good about their products and they want you to *feel good when you buy their products.*

Then they want you to come back and buy more. And they want you to tell your friends about their great products (with the plan that your friends will get on board and start the process all over again).

Everyone in the chain keeps buying their products, is happy to do so, and talks about their products and how much they like: the Nike gym shoes and workout wear, the Coca-Cola, the BMW, and the Hershey's chocolate.

That is good branding.

So, back to you!

Similar to how the four examples of product brands work with their "audience" (also known as their "target market") to create customers who "buy" and are happy with their products, in the same manner, you have an "audience" out there. You want them to "buy" your work (such as when they hire you) and you want them to be happy with their "purchase."

The *personal branding* part comes into play when you work at building your personal brand and communicating it to the "world," where you will one day earn a living.

Building your personal brand involves:

- Defining and analyzing your target market
- Analyzing yourself
- Analyzing your competitors
- Analyzing your visual identity
- Analyzing your verbal identity
- Creating a brand message
- Implementing a visibility plan

Once you develop your personal brand, it doesn't stop there! As time goes on and you make adjustments to your career path, you will also adjust your personal brand. Therefore, keep any work you do on your brand and store it where you can easily retrieve it later. Tweak it when necessary. It will help you for many years to come as you reflect on your career to a point and determine where you want to go next. Your "adjusted" personal brand will continue to serve you successfully until you retire!

Retire?

Okay, maybe we're getting ahead of ourselves. Let's get back to what you're facing *now*, as a college student, as you face your first full-time job (your entryway to the career world) in just a year or two (or less!).

Let me also mention—some people say that *branding yourself* **only** has to do with your participation in social media. I disagree with that. While social media can be a part of your personal branding, it is just that—only a *part*. (The rest of the *parts* are in this book!)

If you're counting on your personal brand to be what people read on your blog, LinkedIn, and perhaps another site or two, keep in mind that your online presence is more like an *online résumé*. It's you on *digital* paper.

However, your personal brand is about much more than that.

In the rest of the chapters you'll learn about all aspects of your personal brand: How you can build it, how you can use it to get positive attention for a job offer, and how you can continue to use it throughout your career to be as successful as possible.

As you read, it might help to write your ideas in either a spiral notebook, in Word, or in some other format. **If this is your book, write notes in it.** Keep whatever notes you write over time so that you can come back to it.

Here is another idea: The first time you read through the book, decide whether you want to do the exercises as you read it *or* read through it the first time without doing the exercises and come back later to do them. Either way is fine.

Are you ready? Let's build a personal brand that is authentic, and that helps you get the interview, get the job, and get the career success you want!

You Actually Have "Customers"!

When new products are developed, the future *customer* for any given product is kept in mind throughout the development process. Whether the product is spaghetti, chocolate, a football, or a car, product brand managers constantly keep everything about the product focused on their future customers.

Some products, such as spaghetti and chocolate, have "mass appeal," in that a broad spectrum of people will buy the product: all ages, men and women, all socioeconomic levels.

For other products, such as footballs and cars, there will be "niche appeal." Footballs will have customers who play the game (or parents of children who play the game). Specific car models are always intended for certain groups of people that include a combination of categories based on age, education, gender, and socioeconomic status.

When products are branded to sell to the public, the brand managers figure out *who* is going to buy the products and then they analyze those potential buyers: Who are they? What do they like? What are their demographics? The potential buyers are called the *target market*.

When *you* are the brand, you also have a target market. They are the people who *buy you*, so to speak, by offering you a job and paying you money to perform that job. So, you need to know something about these "buyers" before you approach them with a résumé and before your interview. Then, as your career goes forward, you'll need to update your target market for how people and circumstances change over time.

When you've had jobs in the past, the people who hired you were your target market customer (at that time). There was something about you they were looking for in an employee, and they believed they found that "something" in you when they offered you the job.

For your post graduation job in your career field, the hiring managers will typically have certain characteristics in common with one another.

Have you met any people lately who could be considered to be *like* your target market? For example, perhaps you've met some managers (in your previous jobs) who are similar to the types of managers who will offer you a job in the future.

Or maybe your parents, your uncles and aunts, and some of your parents' neighbors are similar to the very people who will soon become your boss.

This is important to consider, even while you're still in college.

If you're not coming up with any ideas, you've got some pre-work to do. That is, you can start asking people the following:

> "My career field is *abcxyz*.... What do you think
> the hiring managers in this field are like?"

Here are some examples of the people you can ask: Other students who graduated before you and got a job in either the same or a similar field; professors; your parents; your parents' neighbors; other relatives; people you've met in other activities. I'm referring to people who are older than 22, who are professionals, and who have a good idea about your career field. For example, if your uncle is an attorney, but you're going into engineering, he might still have a good idea of what hiring managers in your field are like. As another example, if one of your neighbors is a corporate accountant, but you're majoring in economics, he or she will probably have a good idea of what your hiring managers are like, too. The more people you ask, the better.

Brainstorm a list of all the people you want to ask. (By the way, you'll get more information by talking to people about this than you will from e-mail or text because you can ask them to clarify their ideas while you have them on the phone or in person. Or, you can send out e-mails asking the question, and if their response makes you want to know more, ask for a time to call them.)

Make a list of all of the responses you get. Weed out the descriptions that just don't sound right to you (or set them aside). If you kept hearing similar phrases regarding what they think your future hiring managers are like, you've hit on some key descriptions of what other people think about your target market managers. You'll also learn from this exercise that some people are very observant of others and good at giving you a thorough description. On the other hand, some people are not very observant or as aware of others as you might have thought, or they have a hard time describing people to you. That's why you'll want to include a lot of people in this "poll."

When you identify common themes and descriptions regarding what your target market people are *like,* you can start to look around you and determine *who you know now* who is similar to them.

(Think about it....) Who is your target market similar to? Who is in your life now that is like them? List their names. (Maybe your uncle, the attorney, is a lot like the hiring managers in your field–even if you're not going into law. We're just looking for similarities at this point.)

Once you have a list of names, for each of them (or for all of them as a group, if they are all very similar), analyze them. Figure out and list the qualities about them that are important to them. For example:

What do they look for in an employee?

_____

_____

_____

What qualities in an employee would bother them?

_____

_____

_____

What catches their attention?

_____

_____

_____

What do they value?

_____

_____

_____

Write down everything you figure out about these people.

_____

_____

_____

After you have defined and analyzed the people you know (and know of) who are similar to your target market, read through all you have written. Do you see any themes that are consistent? What stands out to you?

Once you get closer to graduation and are seeking a job, you will need to identify your target market people more specifically. As you get their names, consider who knows these people. Can you find out more about them? Or is what you already figured out about them (by analyzing people who are similar to them) enough?

In the future, after you've started your first job, there will be other people at your company who can offer you a different job or project. Those people will also become part of your target market. Go through the same analysis with these managers. This time, though, you will know who these people are by name. You can focus your target market analysis specifically on them.

When you're at the point that you've discovered what is important to your target market people (i.e. you've answered most of the previous questions), you can compare that to your own strengths and preferences.

If it seems too early for you to answer these questions, in the next chapter you'll analyze yourself. If you need to, come back to the set of questions below later, after you've read the next chapter.

Where do your target markets' values line up well with your own values, strengths, preferences, and priorities?

_____

_____

_____

Where do they *not* line up well with your own values, strengths, preferences, and priorities?

_____

_____

_____

From what you wrote in response to the previous question, what do you think you can change so that you're both happy?

_____

_____

_____

If you're finding some conflict between your target market's values, preferences, etc. and yours, here are three other ideas:

- Adjust your priorities/preferences.
- Find a different target market set of people to work with in your career.
- Set long-term goals, such as learning as much as you can when you're in your 20s about your field from your target market people (even though your values don't line up). Then, in your 30s, plan for how you will set out on your own (such as in your own business) or make a career change that involves a new target market whose values equal your values.

It's tough to discover that the target market for your chosen career field values work (or something else in the world) differently than you do. You can change your career over time, however, and find a target market that "buys" what you're "selling," and everyone is happy.

For a huge majority of you, the target market hiring managers in your career field will be fine for you to work for over time. Getting a good idea of who they are, what they like, what bothers them, and what they're looking for in a new employee will help you figure out how your personal brand will appeal to them when they're ready to hire.

Sum It Up

- ☑ It's important when branding yourself to figure out who is in your target market.
- ☑ If you're not sure what catches the attention of your target market, what is important to them, or what they value, you have more analysis work to do in order to figure it out. Start asking the "thoughtful" people you know to help you brainstorm.

☑ A way to find out more about your target market is to list people who know them who are more accessible. Figure out ways to speak with those people about what your target market reads, values, is annoyed by, and is impressed by.

☑ If you can speak directly to people in your target market about anything that helps you analyze them further, do it!

☑ After doing some analysis on your target market, summarize what they value in business and in business people.

☑ Tie together your thoughts about your self-brand so far with whatever your target market values. Look for synergy.

Figure Out How Others See You: Will It Help You or Not?

When you think about *who you are* and *what you offer the world*, what comes to mind?

Did you think of positive things you offer the world? Or did any negative things come to mind?

If anything negative came to mind, those will fall into two groups. The first is "things to work on." We all have those and you'll get to work on it as you work on your personal brand. The second group includes negative things people have said that were just cruel. These can replay over and over in your thoughts. Those types of thoughts need to leave. This is not the time to let old messages from negative people (such as their criticisms) take up brain-space in your head. Do what you have to do to put those past you.

For the most part, though, we're going to focus a lot on everything positive about you.

- What do you know about yourself (including traits, characteristics, and skills) that you'll bring to the workplace?
- What do you dream can be possible in your career?
- What is different about you (in a good way)?
- What do you bring to the table that others don't?
- What experiences do you have?
- What skills have you gained over time?

Why Is This Important for College Students?

When working on your personal brand, *analyzing yourself* is an important step for everyone. It's especially important for college students, however.

For the reasons noted in the first chapter, many "things" happen in the lives of college students that have become easy to find out about and, thanks to the Internet, those "things" don't go away (or they don't go away easily). Students get in trouble, get involved in pranks, or have compromising pictures of themselves along with their names posted on web pages. As mentioned earlier, this is more of an "early 20s" issue, and will continue to plague future generations of college students.

My uncle spent a couple years at the college I attended, many years before I arrived. The pranks he and his classmates pulled were just that–pranks. They didn't hurt anyone or hurt property. Their stunts were actually funny. And no one would be embarrassed by the types of things they did if those pranks were reported in the school or town newspapers.

When I went to school there, some guys still pulled pranks. Others destroyed property–which was really stupid. Like breaking-the-law-stupid. If their stupid "things" wound up in the newspaper, I don't recall. But even if it was reported along with students' names, those newspapers are stored in an archive somewhere. You can't pull up those stories on the Internet. If you were going to employ any of the guys involved in setting my school's bell tower on fire, you wouldn't be able to find the story of their stupidity connected with their names. Lucky for them.

Not so lucky for people born after 1980. For people born after that year, the chances are if you break the law, damage property, or get involved in anything I've called "stupid" and it winds up in the college or town newspaper, the text will be available on the Internet for anyone to find.

Let's go back to something you read earlier in the first chapter.

About 2007, we started hearing reports of 27-year-olds who were interviewing for jobs, only to find out that the prospective employers searched the Internet for anything available about them. Those same young adults contacted their alma maters requesting the schools to take down articles from their newspaper's online web pages that told stories about (say it with me) "stupid things" they did while they were students.

Did the schools comply? No way. The schools refused to remove the less-than-attractive articles from their websites.

Now, don't think you're "okay" just because you have a common name that is shared by thousands of people. By just adding your college or university to the search criteria, company representatives can easily narrow down their search and find you.

At this point, I have two audiences reading this book:

- Students who've already committed the "stupid" (which may or may not be available on the Internet)
- Students who have not done anything remotely stupid (so far)

Regardless which group you fall into, I have a message for both of you. (You might even call it a *plan*.)

What is "Stupid"?

Let's go over a list that, while not comprehensive, gives you an idea of the types of "things" you don't want to do that a prospective employer may be able to find later (and then choose not to hire you):

- Get a DUI
- Destroy property
- Get a lot of traffic tickets (to the point of losing your license)
- Get in a fight to which police are called

- Allow compromising pictures to be taken of yourself
- (This list is *not* comprehensive, as you read above!)

I'm going to deal with some of those "things" here.

Any time you drink too much, it can lead to problems. Even if you don't get into the driver's seat of a car, drinking too much can lead to making poor choices, such as getting into fights, destroying property, or not realizing that someone is taking a picture of you.

Ladies, *the pictures!* Your *personal branding problems* often center on this one. Do you know how many unflattering pictures are on Facebook, tagged with peoples' names? I don't know how many, either, but it's a lot. You don't want an unflattering or compromising picture of yourself to be anywhere on the Internet. And that goes for any digital picture taken with a cell phone or digital camera. Those can wind up anywhere.

A youth leader who works with college students once told me about a group of girls at a sorority who took *more-than-sexy* photos of each other. The town newspaper found out and wrote an article about it. *Um, this is a really bad idea.* What seemed funny at the time may have implications for these girls for years, depending on whether the article mentioned names.

But what if the newspaper article didn't mention names? Even if the article appeared on the newspaper's website, if it didn't have names mentioned in it, who cares?

Well, let's talk about blogs. How many students do you know who write a blog? Maybe after reading the article in the newspaper, other students blogged about it and used the girls' names. Hmmm. There we go again. It's available on the Internet via a simple search for as long as that blog is searchable.

Or maybe they Tweeted it with a link to the blog. (Tweets are not necessarily private. You can elect to protect your tweets but, as of this writing, they are only protected after you turn on the setting.) Also, someone who follows you may not protect their tweets. Or they might tweet about something you did, use your name in a tweet, etc. (I'm telling you this about Twitter after I Googled my niece's name and easily found her tweets.)

What do you do if there is already an unflattering photo, article, or blog about you in cyberspace?

I suggest locating the source first. Who posted the photo, article, or blog? If you're still a student, you may be able to get it taken down or untagged. (When you're 27, you may be out of luck.) If the person refuses to take it down (or untag it) when you ask them, will your parents help you by making the request on your behalf? If not, is there some other adult who might be willing to help you?

Any choice you make (or comment someone writes about you) can be listed somewhere on the Internet at any time. And, thanks to blogs and social networking sites, stories can be added long after the actual event occurred. In fact, one of your Facebook friends can copy private text and paste it to another site that is not private.

Many people feel that their information is well-protected on social media sites where you can control the privacy settings. But privacy experts have warned for years that it's easy to get a false sense of security from these sites. Any information that is online can easily be copied by someone who has access, and then pasted elsewhere.

Privacy settings and privacy software change every few months. To that point, people and companies who want to get around privacy settings (in order to find you anyway) are working at their findings just as quickly. Stay informed in order to protect yourself.

In order to keep up with any bad news that might show up on the Internet about you, here are the actions you can take:

1. The first is the most obvious. Check your favorite search engine (Google, Yahoo, etc.) for your name and type it with double quotation marks (i.e. "Glory Borgeson"). See what is out there now for the first four

pages of results. If your name is common, also type your name with your middle initial. For another search, after typing your name in double quotation marks, type the name of your school outside the quotation marks.

Does anything come up that you're concerned about? If so, print out the page (or section of the page). Copy the URL from the address box and paste it into a Word document so that you can easily find that page again. Save the Word document with all of your notes and links. Talk with trusted adults regarding how to request the negative information to be removed. (The source might refuse you, but you can try!)

Another site to try is Snitch.name. This URL pulls data from many different sites at one time. Try it by typing in your name and see what comes up. Then try a friend's name. This is a site that many employers will use to check out applicants. (Also try PeekYou.com and Spokeo.com.)

2. This is a great way to keep up with new entries about you that appear on the Internet: Google Alerts.

Go to: www.Google.com/Alerts

Set up a Google Alert on your name. In the "Search Terms" box, type your name in double quotation marks (i.e. "John Doe"). You can also create a second Alert including your middle initial. Keep the "Type" as "Comprehensive," and for "How Often" choose how often you want to receive the Alert e-mails. Enter your e-mail address and click the "Create Alert" button. (Google Alerts was still in BETA as of this writing. If it looks different on your screen, follow Google's instructions to create the Alert.)

You will then receive e-mails alerting you every time something new appears on the Internet with your name. Check out each new listing. If the news is negative, follow the instructions in the previous point.

3. Check out your friends' pages on social networking sites regularly. Is your name shown in a negative way? Are there any pictures of you that should be removed? Talk to your friend and request them to remove the negative text or pictures. If you need to, get a trusted adult to help you.

How Do Other People "See" You?

Matt is a senior in college, majoring in marketing, and he's planning to get a job in sales. Two friends of his, Mike and Bill, are also seniors, majoring in computer science and secondary education, respectively. At a *Brand Yourself!* seminar I conducted at their school, I did an exercise that, while fun (and often funny), shows how well *we think* others see ourselves.

I gave each of the guys (as well as the audience) a list of personal traits that cover just about all personal traits. I told the audience to list two friends' names and then, for each friend, go through the list and choose the top 5 traits they believed described each friend pretty well. (Matt, Mike, and Bill did this for each other.)

When they were done with the five traits for each friend, I told them to list the top five traits they believe described *themselves.*

Next, I invited Matt, Mike, and Bill to the front of the room. Singling out Matt, I asked Mike and Bill to tell me the five traits each of them listed for Matt, and I wrote those on a flipchart. Many times, two people who know the same friend in the same setting (such as at college) will describe that friend similarly.

Then I asked Matt to tell us the five traits he listed for himself.

This is where it gets interesting. And I never know what I'm going to get as a result.

If Matt's five traits for himself are quite close to the traits his friends listed for him, it means he sees himself closely to how other people see him (or at least to how *his friends* see him).

If Matt's five traits for himself are different from what his friends chose, it means he has a *lack of awareness* of how others view him.

Doing this "test" with your friends is one singular level. An even more interesting experiment would be to do this with people you've worked with before at previous jobs. How would your boss and co-workers choose your traits? Would they choose traits that would be close to what you would choose for yourself?

Try this exercise with two friends. Using the following list of character traits as a start, ask them to select *all* of your qualities and character traits. Next, out of the entire list of traits they selected, they should choose the *top five* that they believe really describe you. (Your two friends should work on their own list separately, not together.)

As part of this exercise, you also make your own list of your qualities and character traits, as you see yourself, and then choose what you believe are the top five. (You might even have one list that you believe describes you when you're with friends, and a second list that describes you when you're at work.)

Last, compare your two friends' lists (of the five traits) to each other. Then compare your list to theirs. How close did you come to how they see you? What does the result tell you?

On the opposite page is a list of character traits to start with. If you can think of more, add them to this list.

Active	Curious	Generous	Naïve
Adventurous	Daring	Gentle	Negligent
Affable	Dauntless	Giving	Nervous
Affectionate	Decisive	Glamorous	Obedient
Ambitious	Dependable	Grateful	Obliging
Amiable	Determined	Gullible	Optimistic
Animated	Diligent	Happy	Peaceful
Annoyed	Discouraged	Harried	Persevering
Anxious	Discreet	Helpful	Persistent
Attentive	Dismayed	Honest	Polite
Blasé	Disrespectful	Hopeful	Popular
Bored	Dissatisfied	Hopeless	Proud
Brave	Distressed	Hospitable	Quick
Brilliant	Doubtful	Humble	Rational
Busy	Dutiful	Humorous	Refined
Calm	Eager	Imaginative	Reliable
Candid	Easygoing	Immature	Respectful
Capable	Effervescent	Impartial	Responsible
Careful	Efficient	Impatient	Responsive
Caustic	Eloquent	Impudent	Rowdy
Cautious	Encouraging	Impulsive	Safe
Charismatic	Energetic	Independent	Sarcastic
Charming	Enthusiastic	Industrious	Secure
Cheerful	Exacting	Innocent	Sincere
Clever	Excited	Insistent	Smart
Compassionate	Expert	Intelligent	Sociable
Complacent	Exuberant	Jealous	Stubborn
Concerned	Fair	Lackadaisical	Thoughtful
Confident	Faithful	Lively	Thrifty
Conscientious	Fearless	Logical	Tolerant
Considerate	Fidgety	Loving	Trusting
Cooperative	Finicky	Loyal	Trustworthy
Courageous	Foolish	Mature	Unselfish
Cowardly	Formal	Meticulous	Warmhearted
Crafty	Fortunate	Mischievous	Wise
Critical	Frank	Moody	Witty
Cultured	Friendly	Mysterious	Worried

I left out many traits that have negative connotations from the list above. If you want a really full list of these, use your favorite search engine to look up "character traits." Remember that once you're in the workplace in your first job, your boss will come up with his or her list *for you* (in their mind) which may include *negative traits*. Part of your *personal branding* work will involve branding yourself so well that your boss (and others at the company) brand you *as you want to be branded* instead of with some random set of traits that may include negative traits.

If there is some way you can ask former bosses and co-workers to do the same exercise regarding *your* character traits, go ahead and send them an e-mail or give them a call first. (If they can e-mail their list to you, that is best.) How close do you come to analyzing yourself as compared to people you've worked with doing the same exercise? What does the result tell you?

If your analysis of yourself is close to the others' evaluation, you see yourself closely to how others see you. If your analysis looks very different, you'll need to make some adjustments to your brand.

When your list comes out *different* from others' lists for you, ask yourself:

- Would I prefer to be known for the qualities and character traits on my list?
  Or –
- Would I prefer to be known for the qualities and character traits on another person's list?

Your Own List

If you prefer to be known by what is on your own list, your *personal branding* work will involve tweaking how you present yourself to the world (especially in the workplace) so that others' perception of you changes to reflect your list.

Another Person's List

If you prefer to be known by what is on someone else's list, your *personal branding* work will involve tweaking how you see yourself so that your brand reflects that other person's list.

As you continue to read the other chapters, you will go through additional exercises that pull you toward building your personal brand. As you do so, keep in mind which "list" you want to be known for as you start your career.

Sum It Up

- ✔ *Analyzing yourself* is an important part of building your personal brand.
- ✔ If your unwise youthful choices wind up in a newspaper or on someone's blog, it can be found by potential employers with a simple Internet search.
- ✔ Employers who find negative information about a job candidate usually do not offer the job to that person.
- ✔ It can be difficult to get negative information about yourself removed from the Internet, but it doesn't hurt to try.
- ✔ Find out how other people "see" you in terms of your personal traits, characteristics, and skills, and compare that to how you "see" yourself.
- ✔ Determine how you actually *want* others to "see" your personal traits, characteristics, and skills.

Many People Want the Same Job as You Want: How Can You Win?

Honda wants you to buy a Civic. Nissan wants you to buy a Sentra. Dell wants you to buy their PC. Apple wants you to buy their Mac. Coke vs. Pepsi. Nike vs. Adidas. Hershey's vs. Nestlé.

These brands have competitors. *You* have competitors.

These brands want you to buy their product over their competition.

You want your #1 company choice/hiring manager to choose you over your competition.

Your competitors are people who want the same interview you want, the same job you want, the same raises you want, and the same promotions you want.

Sometimes, you will know who your competitors are by name. When you're already employed at a company and a position opens up for which the company will first look to fill from within the firm, you may know some of your fellow competitors since you will all work at the same company.

If you're going for a job where you don't already work, you won't personally know your competitors. However, you will know *about* them. They will have a degree and major similar to yours. They will have a similar intelligence level. They might have similar skill sets.

In chapter one, you read about stories that have been in the press about immature behaviors people in their 20s do on the job (and how unhappy that makes their managers).

I also stated there:

You might be thinking, "That's not fair. I'm not like that. I don't act like that."

You may be thinking the truth. Unfortunately, the burden is on you to prove it. Fortunately, you can do that by branding yourself well.

By analyzing your competition, you can begin to distinguish your brand from *their* brand. If "others" are the people who are acting immaturely in the workplace, then one of the things you can do to distinguish yourself in a positive light with your target market is to *act maturely*.

From the stories I hear from managers about their experiences working with people in their 20s, you would wonder why more of the younger employees don't see these circumstances as an opportunity to edge people out and get (take?) the job over their immature counterparts.

Here is a case in point:

Carol is an occupational therapist. She told me a story about being in management at a clinic in a southern state. One of her employees (I'll call her Mary) was 26 years old and also an occupational therapist. For this field, people need a master's degree–it's definitely a professional position. One day, Mary didn't show up for work. Didn't call. Nothing. Of course, Carol and her staff were concerned about her, so Carol called her at home. Mary answered the phone and said she was sick. Carol asked why Mary didn't call in the morning to inform the staff she wouldn't be in the clinic because she was sick. Mary said the last place she worked didn't require employees to call in sick. Carol, wondering why she would need to explain this to an adult, told Mary she needed to call the clinic early in the morning on any day she's sick. And besides, Carol reminded her, Mary had patient appointments all day that needed to be rescheduled.

On another occasion, Mary called the clinic one morning to say she had been at a party at a hotel the night before with her boyfriend, they had a fight, and he left her there stranded without transportation. Mary wondered if someone from work could pick her up. (As Carol said to me, "That would have been a good time to just call in sick rather than tell us that story.")

I hear stories like this regularly.

Interview Faux Pas

Since much of your competition will be ruled out during their interview, let's review some actual *things* (that's the only way to describe these words or actions) young interviewees have done during an interview that you can call your "Don'ts". (We'll also review more "Don'ts" in the chapter about your verbal brand.) Below, the action taken by the interviewee is listed first. My comment following is in italics.

- Taking snacks out of your briefcase or backpack during the interview and eating.

  The only ingesting you may do during an interview is to drink the water, coffee, or tea you were offered before the interview began.

- Cell phone rings–he looks at the phone to see who's calling.

  If you forget to turn off your cell phone (and I do mean turn it off; don't put it on vibrate), apologize and turn it off right away, without looking to see who called.

- Asking the interviewer if he is Jewish (or Christian or Buddhist or Muslim, etc.)

  This interviewee may have thought she would make a

connection with the interviewer with that question, but she just turned off the interviewer. You are better off not asking the interviewer these types of personal questions.

- Repeating the same phrase multiple times, such as, "At the end of the day."
  Practice what you are going to say in the interview. See the chapter titled "Will the Way You Speak and Write Help You Be Successful?" to find out more about that to keep your speech "normal."

- Nervous tics, such as a bouncing leg.
  Again, practice ahead of time. Consciously take breaths to control your nervousness.

- Saying too much about certain topics (or anything at all), such as discussing family problems, credit problems, boyfriend/girlfriend problems, upcoming planned vacation for which you need time off, etc.
  "Less is more" where personal information is concerned during your interview.

- Dressing inappropriately for the interview.
  See the chapter titled, "Will the Way You Look Help You Be Successful?"

- Saying, "I haven't had a chance to look at your company's website yet."
  Why should this company be interested in you if you haven't been very interested in them?

- Being unaware of what is "out there" on the Internet about you, and not cleaning it up.
  You read about this in the previous chapter, "Figure Out How Others See You: Will It Help You or Not?"

- Not looking the interviewer in the eye.
  Can you believe there are 22-year-olds who still don't look other adults in the eye? I still run into them myself. It is definitely perceived as childish in younger adults. In older adults, not looking people in the eye leads people to believe the individual has something to hide.

- This last point is related to your interview, but has more to do with your résumé. Several hiring managers have told me that they've decided to not interview someone based on their e-mail address (which is displayed on their résumé or on their Monster–or other online–job search listing). If the e-mail address chosen by the interviewee shows a lack of judgment (because it is dirty or childish or silly), they'll probably choose to not interview the person at all.

If you haven't done so yet, go to a free e-mail service and open a business-like e-mail address. You can use your first name and last name, entering a "dot" between each name. If your name is taken, try putting your middle initial in it, with a dot, without a dot, etc., until you find one that isn't taken. One of my relatives once had a personal e-mail address that was something like "pyromaniac" and a number. Not a good e-mail address to use on a résumé or on Monster.

Your competition is doing the types of things (and more– we don't have space here!) listed above during their interviews. They're getting cut from the job prospect list, even if their résumés look great.

You're smarter than that. Rather than get cut from the list, decide what your personal brand is going to portray (and not portray) at the interview.

Much that is written about your age group completing college and entering the workforce talks about your *style* being different from the generations before you and how that is producing conflict. I'll only agree that style is producing a little conflict. But, as you can see, the problem is *not* really style. The problem is immaturity.

If you are viewed ("branded") as immature during the interview (or, later, while in your first job), it is really difficult to undo that.

Much of your competition is acting immaturely–during the interview or, if they ace that, in their first job. If you want to beat your competition, one way you will stand out above the rest is to be mature. Act like a grownup. Do the opposite of what you read in those bullet points above.

Once you have the job, making yourself "shine" as an outstanding employee (i.e. team player, technically excellent in your work, puts in extra effort, etc.) is also important. But if you do those things *and* you also demonstrate immaturity, your bosses will be conflicted about promoting you.

Make *maturity in all things* a top priority. Believe me—much of your competition is not doing that. When I encounter 20-somethings in the workplace who act maturely all the time, it is really refreshing. By their actions, they're telling me that they are responsible, trustworthy, and dependable. That's so much better than the alternative.

Strengths & Weaknesses: Yours and Your Competitor's

Imagine the types of people who are competing for the same jobs as you are. What are *their* strengths? What are *their* weaknesses?

Likewise, what are *your* strengths? What are *your* weaknesses?

How can you position your strengths to beat out your competition's weaknesses?

Your Competition's Strengths

List out what you believe are the strengths that your competition brings to an interview and to the job market:

_____

_____

_____

(Examples: [depending on your field]–intelligence; dedicated worker; multitasker; works well on a team, etc.)

Your Competition's Weaknesses

List out what you believe are your competition's weaknesses, including what you read earlier in chapter one about their immaturity and what you read in this chapter about interview faux pas. What have you figured out about your peers in your chosen field?

_____

_____

_____

(Examples: Chronically late; doesn't care what the boss thinks; spends too much time on personal things while at work; forgets to call when sick; etc.)

Your Strengths

For each of your competition's weaknesses you identified above, think of a strength you have that beats each weakness.

Their Weakness:	Your Corresponding Strength That Beats It:
(Example: Doesn't care if their work is accurate or sloppy)	(Example: Accurate project deliverables, neatly presented)

What do you offer a company as an employee that much of your competition doesn't offer?

_____

_____

_____

_____

Based on what you've written so far, come up with a few *summaries* that describe what you offer that your competition doesn't, or that beats your competition's weaknesses. (These can be short. You'll also work on this at a deeper level in a later chapter.)

_____

_____

_____

_____

Eventually, you'll pull these together in a later chapter. What you offer your future employer is your *value proposition*!

Your value proposition is what you want to keep in mind as you interview, and later, as you work at your first job. It will change over time as you add skill sets to your résumé and figure out more about yourself.

As consumers, we often buy products and services based on the value proposition the selling company came up with in order to sell to us. It tells us something about the product and makes us want to buy. It is part of the branding process that is used to get that value proposition into our minds.

Likewise, as you come up with your own *personal value proposition*, you will want to convey it and get it into the minds of the hiring managers. It starts with how your résumé is worded, and then it extends to how you present yourself in the interview (and, beyond that, how you conduct business once you get the job).

Three examples of statements that serve as a personal value proposition are:

- High sales volume, happy customers
- Accurate accounts, reconciled timely
- Creative designs, team player, dependable project work

Come up with some of your own phrases that highlight what you bring to the table, especially keeping in mind what you do that your competitors tend to not do well.

Keep working on your value proposition below, to come up with better phrases over time:

_____

_____

_____

_____

_____

_____

In the chapter titled "Create a Brand Message that Encompasses Your Brand," you'll work further to expand your brand message so that it demonstrates how you outshine your competition.

Sum It Up

✔ Your competition is anyone who wants the same job you want.

✔ Many of your competitors act very immaturely during interviews and on the job. This drives managers crazy.

✔ Act maturely and you will automatically knock out a huge number of competitors from the job running.

✔ Just as *product* brand managers analyze their competitors' products, you need to determine who your competitors are and analyze their strengths and weaknesses.

✔ Line up your strengths against your competition's weaknesses.

✔ Develop a value proposition based on what you bring to the workforce.

✔ Use your value proposition to beat out your competition and get the job!

✔ Continue to tweak your value proposition over time, throughout your career.

Will the Way You Look
Help You Be Successful?

You go to the store to buy microwave popcorn. Of the various brands on the store shelf, you haven't bought them before or tasted them at someone else's house. You can see five different brands on the shelf, and each brand has three or four different kinds of flavors. You decide you want the kind that's buttered and salted, which is offered by all five.

Within seconds, you decide which one you want. You grab it and head for the checkout. You think to yourself, *This one looks good.*

How do you know it will be good?

You haven't tasted it before.

No one's told you it's the best of those five.

You just guessed it will be good because the *packaging* made it look good to you.

We make quick judgments constantly—about purchases, about movies and TV shows, about a lot of things—and about people.

Likewise, so does everyone else—including interviewers.

People who interview you for jobs are no different than anyone else when it comes to making quick judgments about people. They will make a few quick judgments about you when they first meet you, mostly based on how you look.

Later, after you have the job, your co-workers, bosses, and other colleagues will continue to make quick judgments about you based on how you look. (If it makes you feel any better, they'll do the same to everyone else, too.)

Earlier in the day I was writing this, I was at a client's office in their cafeteria. I saw a man who was probably in his 50s, nicely dressed in business casual attire. When he turned around with his back to me, I noticed that he had tucked a paperback book halfway into his pants. In the first moment, there was just a big question mark in my head, in the form of: "Why would he do that?" and "That looks really weird." In the second moment, I decided he was an engineer. (Sorry to all you engineering students—that's just how it hit me.)

Try this the next time you're meeting new people or at a place where you can people-watch. Try to figure out what they do for a living or, if they're students, what is their major.

Social researchers have found that we tend to make decisions about people within two seconds of meeting them. These two-second *decisions* are in regard to peoples' personalities. We quickly decide whether someone is fun or boring, smart or dumb, someone we'd like to get to know or someone we'd prefer to not talk to at all. We decide this just based on their looks within two seconds!

We might be accurate or we might be completely wrong.

So, since that's the case, you can conclude that many people will make quick decisions about *you* (even if they are wrong!).

In a job interview situation, the interviewer will quickly decide if they think the interviewee would fit into the company or not. This is all based on physical appearance.

If your goal is to get the job, you want your first two seconds with the interviewer to lead their two-second decision about you in a positive direction. Your looks, from head to toe, will be scrutinized quickly.

It's important that you have your "look" put together before you interview for jobs.

You don't have to dress like people in their 40s, your parents, or your grandparents. You can dress like a 20-something business-oriented adult. Also, you don't have to look like you're wearing a uniform.

Recently, a friend described a group of college seniors who were interviewing for a sales position at a large, well-known firm. Her boss, a man in his 50s, whispered to my friend, "They all look alike!" She looked around and realized all of the interviewees were dressed alike, making it look like they were wearing uniforms: Black suit, white shirt or blouse, and similar looking ties for the men.

The point is, you don't have to look identical to the others. The important thing is to dress the part and to show respect. By that I mean—if you research how the younger adults who work at the particular company dress (and, maybe, in the particular department for which you are interviewing) and then you put that "look" together for yourself, you show *respect* for the people conducting your interview.

Developing your "look" (or your personal brand's "*visual identity*") is something you will tweak throughout your career, as you change careers and as styles change. Keep this in mind when you *rethink* your personal brand every few years.

Your "look" includes your clothing and shoes, the accessories you wear (glasses, watch, other jewelry), your hairstyle, how you smell, your posture, and how you walk.

Your "Visual Brand" for the Interview

Interviews are *not* the place to demonstrate your individuality.

Unless you're in a really creative field (where "crazier is better"), keep your "interview look" to something that errs on the side of conservative. However you envision people dress at the company where you're interviewing, dress a little "quieter" than that.

We've already covered a few important aspects of creating your "look" for the interview–and that continues below for men, women, and for both of you.

Before going any further, I want you to consider one other aspect of "interviewing" that occurs before you even sit down with an interviewer.

Consider this: You might encounter people (*before* you even interview for your first job) who are able to refer you for interviews and job possibilities when you're not even thinking about it. These are very important people. If you don't *look the part* in this person's eyes (and within two seconds), they probably won't even mention their connection to a possible great job for you.

Who are these people? They are your parents' friends, neighbors, your former employers, etc. They are all kinds of adults who have connections that you don't necessarily know about. And they can make good connections for you to great job possibilities.

It's important to start *looking the part* in your junior and senior years whenever you're around adults. You never know who can help you get that first great job!

That means, even when you're dressed casually, pay attention to what you're wearing and how you're wearing it.

When you're just out seeing adults you've known for years (such as you parents' friends and people you know in your hometown), or just at a store in town where you might bump into adults you know, here is a "Do" and "Don't" list, including what that adult is thinking if you're "wearing" what is in that list:

"I've Got to Get that Student in for an Interview" (or...Make an Introduction...)	"Forget it—He or She Doesn't Look the Part for that Company/Job/etc."
● Clean t-shirt (not torn) ● Well-fitting jeans or shorts ● Shoes or flip flops that aren't falling apart ● If a tattoo is showing, something that would be covered by clothes in a real interview ● Modest jewelry (or, for men, no jewelry)	● Body jewelry and piercings ● Odd jewelry ● T-shirt with an obscene graphic or words ● Jeans or shorts that show your underwear, derriér, or too much skin ● Mohawk hair style or strange colored hair ● Large (or obnoxious) tattoos

As you get closer to graduation and you're around adults who might be able to make a job connection or recommend you for a position, even when you're not actually interviewing–you're prospecting for interviews!

For the Men

For the guys, your interview clothing will usually mean a suit and tie (even if you know that everyone dresses in business casual every day at that office). If your contact person at the company specifically tells you to dress casually for your interview, then you can wear a button-down shirt and casual trousers. If they don't say anything about how you should dress, then go for the suit and tie. And that means a "quiet" tie. Someone asked me to define a "quiet" tie. That is a tie with standard colors and patterns. No bright colors. No neon colors. No "Three Stooges" ties (my brother has one of those that he wears for sales calls). On your part, this demonstrates respect for the people you're meeting at your interview. If you don't own a decent pair of dress shoes, go out and buy a pair that work well with your suit. A lot of women notice men's shoes, too. It's a good idea to own a pair of dress shoes. And, please, make sure your socks coordinate with the suit and shoes.

A client of mine had a 23-year-old MBA in their office who wore a beautiful diamond ring–kind of surprising for a guy his age. I found out that while he was in college, he worked at a jewelry store and bought the ring with his employee discount. Still, for his age, I recommended that he not wear the ring on job interviews. It stood out too much on him. (If he were in his 40s or 50s, it would have been fine. But not at 23.)

For jewelry, a watch is enough. Possibly a ring–a wedding ring if you're married; a class ring is also okay. Leave everything else at home. No earrings. No other facial piercings showing. No necklace. No bracelet. No other rings.

If you're still wearing the "I'm in college" hairstyle, look around at guys who are a little older than you are–and already in the workplace–for the types of hairstyles they're wearing. And then go get a haircut so that you fit in.

As for facial hair, a beard is not a good idea for most types of job interviews. Right now, moustaches are not in style. (If they come back in style, then a moustache is okay.) Also, as I write, goatees are in style, but not really for guys your age. We mostly see them now on guys who are over 30. But if you are 22 and have a young look (some would call it a "baby face"), then you might be able to get away with a goatee and make yourself look older. Ask a few men who are between 35 and 50 if they think you should keep the goatee or get rid of it before your interview.

That brings me to the "smell" part. Don't wear cologne or aftershave. You never know if the person conducting the interview has a sensitivity to cologne or doesn't like your cologne. Go with the "just showered" smell and you'll be good in the "scent" department. (And, if you smoke, don't let nervousness about the interview make you light up on your drive over to the interview. You don't want to smell like tobacco.)

For the Women

Ladies, similar to the guys, you'll usually want to wear a suit to your interview. You have more choices about which blouse or sweater to wear with it, such as color. Bolder colors for a blouse are okay (more than they used to be for an interview). Just don't wear neon-type colors or crazy prints. For the suit, go with neutrals, such as black, navy, olive, tan, or, in warmer weather, pastels.

Just don't wear anything too tightly fitting; and please, I beg of you, don't come close to showing any cleavage. Or belly. Or back skin. Women interviewers will cross you right off the list of job candidates. (And the male interviewers–well –you don't want to be hired because you showed too much skin. That's not a personal brand you really want for yourself.)

Make certain your shoes coordinate with your outfit. Only wear boots if it's winter and you can't get around it. If you choose to wear a dress or skirt instead of slacks, it's not a good idea to go bare-legged into an interview. If you just never wear hosiery, wear a pantsuit.

Women can get away with wearing more jewelry to an interview than men. Earrings, a simple necklace, a simple bracelet, and one or two rings work well. Just like with the men: *No other facial piercings.*

Most women who are 21 or 22 years old seem to have hairstyles similar to women who are 28 years old, so you should be okay with your hair. Ask a woman who is a few years older than you are about how women in their 20s are wearing their hair at work. If it's pretty much like yours, you're good.

Just like with the men, don't wear cologne. You just never know if someone conducting the interview won't like the scent of your cologne and will cross your name off the list. And this bears repeating: If you smoke, don't let nervousness about the interview make you light up on your drive over to the interview. You don't want to smell like tobacco.

For All of You

I've learned that people in their early 20s are not wearing watches like their older counterparts. You use your cell phone to tell you the time. Boomers and some older Gen-X-er's don't understand it. Probably because it takes more time to pull out your cell phone than it does to glance at your watch.

So I'm going to give you the answer to the *Why wear a watch to my interview?* question that a few of you are wondering. *Because it shows respect.* We older folks who interview you want to know that *being on time for the interview* is important to you and, therefore, you wore a watch on your interview day so that you would not be late. It's a nice touch. Borrow a good looking watch if you don't own one. It doesn't have to be expensive—just professional looking.

That brings me to tattoos. Studies have shown that people whose tattoos were visible during a job interview were less likely to get the job offer than people who did not have any visible tattoos. Hopefully, you don't have a tattoo on your hands, face, or upper neck. Those should be your only exposed areas. If you have a tattoo on your forearm, wear long sleeves. I mean it.

Like I mentioned earlier, if you're in a more creative field where everyone dresses "out there," you can be more edgy than I've described. Use your best judgment. About 90 percent of you I meet, however, are not in a super creative career field.

Your "Visual Brand" After You Get the Job

After you get your first job, your *personal branding* work continues.

You don't have to dress like your parents. Instead, once you're in your job, pay attention to how the people dress who are between 25 and 35, for those in that age category who you also notice are *respected by others* (especially by the bosses). How do they dress? How much jewelry do they wear? If the office has a casual day (or if every day is casual attire), what do they wear (and how do they wear it) so as not to come across as sloppy or too young?

If you wear cologne, go ahead and wear it. Just don't wear a lot. (I have a sensitivity to one brand of women's cologne and you would not believe how many women wear that brand. Ugh.)

Ladies, still don't wear clothes that are too tight fitting or show cleavage, belly, or back skin. Some of the guys might like it, but it will not get you the respect you need to get future promotions.

It takes time to build a work wardrobe. Find out which stores sell work attire for your age group and give you the best value. That doesn't mean to "buy cheap." It means to locate the stores with the best sales so that you can buy the best quality possible within your budget.

If you're a guy, ask around to find these stores. (You girls usually already know where to shop. If you're in a new town, though, ask around.)

You might think you're saving time by shopping online. However, returning clothes and shoes that don't fit well can be a hassle. (One exception, as of this writing, is Zappos.com, which makes returns easy because you don't pay to ship items back; Zappos pays. But you still have to prepare the items to return.)

If boxing up clothes that don't fit and sending them back seems like a hassle to you, go to stores and try clothes on.

You'll usually save more time overall by going to the stores that sell the type of clothes you need for work, trying them on, and buying only the items that fit well.

If you're not the "clothes-type," ask a friend who has a good sense of style to help you. That person will also know the best places to shop. Yes, *go shopping.*

Besides clothing and shoes, consider other things, such as accessories (including jewelry, glasses, computer bag or case, briefcase [or something like it], handbag), and your hairstyle. Again, look around at your co-workers who are between 25 and 35 who appear to be respected by management and see which accessories they wear, how they style their hair, and make choices for yourself that fit in.

The point is to keep your individuality without being the odd-person-out who just looks immature.

Take a Visual Inventory of Yourself

Taking a visual inventory is a good thing to do every five years or so. Styles change, jobs change, bosses change, and *you change.*

When it's time for you to take a visual inventory, go through the questions on the next page and answer for where you are today (where it says "You Today"), and also answer (in the far right column) for someone you know (or know of) who is successful and who you admire.

	You Today	Someone Else Who is Successful
● What are your (their) best features?		
● What are your (their) worst features		
● Describe your (their) posture		
● Describe how you (they) walk		
● Describe the clothing you (they) wear to work		
● Describe the accessories you (they) wear (or bring) to work		
● Describe your (their) hairstyle		

Next, go through the "You" column answers. What would you like to keep? What would you like to change?

Last, go through the column on the far right, for the other successful person. What could you "borrow" from that person that you could add to your "look"? What would it take for you to make those changes?

Pull It Together

From what you've read so far, consider what you're going to keep and what you're going to change about your visual presence in the workplace.

If it helps to write it out, get a piece of paper and jot a few notes (or use whatever you use to take notes). Even write out the visual qualities about yourself that you're going to keep. Seeing it in writing will give you more confidence that the way you appear to people works for you.

Also write out what you're going to change. *Clothing, accessories, hairstyle, shoes, posture, how you walk.* Do any of these stand out as needing to change?

Do you need to buy some new clothes? Figure out how much you can spend every month, and build your *work wardrobe* over time. Don't go into debt over new clothes. Just make a plan and stick to it.

And remember to take a *visual inventory* about every five years. Don't be that person who settles into a "look" when they're 40 years old and never changes it again!

Sum It Up

☑ We humans make quick judgments about peoples' abilities just based on how they look.

☑ People will make quick judgments about *you* based only on how *you* look.

☑ If your goal is to get the job, the decision-maker needs to believe that you *look the part.*

☑ *Looking the part* doesn't mean you look like a 45-year-old; it means that your *look* gives the decision-maker the idea that you are a competent, trustworthy adult who can do the job well and that you are the best candidate for the job.

☑ Your personal branding work doesn't stop when you get your first job. Keep tweaking it every few years.

☑ Taking a visual inventory of yourself will help you see if any changes need to be made in order for the "visual you" to fit the "brand you."

☑ Analyzing the visual identity of a successful person you know and admire will give you ideas about how you might tweak your visual identity to better fit your brand.

☑ Once you've done some analysis, you can start to make visual adjustments to yourself that better communicate *your brand* to your target market (and everyone else!).

Will the Way You Speak and Write Help You Be Successful?

When you decide to buy a product, at some point you will have either heard or read a message about it. Whether you buy soda, a chocolate bar, cologne, a basketball, a bicycle, or a car, chances are you've heard about it or read about it somewhere at some time.

The *communications* about that product (that you've heard or read about) is that product's *verbal identity* that its brand managers wanted you to hear or read in order to convince you to buy it.

And if you bought the product—it worked! Somehow, the product's "verbal identity" spoke to you and persuaded you to buy.

Likewise, your verbal identity comes across in *everything you write* and in *everything you say*.

Your writing at the workplace will include all e-mails, written communications to customers, written presentations, and reports.

Your spoken identity will come across in meetings (formal and informal), in conference calls, and also in casual work conversation.

Written Communications

In the business world, there isn't a whole lot of texting going on regarding business. Mostly, companies use e-mail and phone for communications (and voicemail for spoken messages). Shared databases are used at some companies where employees communicate issues about projects. These communications need to be clear and concise. Not everyone in the workplace understands "texting shorthand." Keep that in mind when communicating in the business world. (As you get older, that may change as the "non-texting adults" retire.)

Business e-mails written with poor grammar reflect poorly on you. Everyone makes "typos" when they're typing quickly–I'm not referring to typos. I'm mentioning writing in business e-mails that would make you seem uneducated because of poor grammar.

Here are a few examples of poorly written business communications:

- "At the meeting, everyone must present there monthly report."
- "When you complete the Smith proposal, please give me a copy to."
- "When the team arrives, their going to meet in room 205."
- "At the meeting, your giving the report results first."

Do you see what is wrong with each of the sentences above? What would be the correct way to write each sentence?

As I was working on this chapter, a 24-year-old guy I know (who is well-educated) wrote me an e-mail asking if I will review his résumé–he's adding his current job to it and needs a second pair of eyes. In his e-mail, he asked me for a meeting, and twice he spelled it "meting." Really!

Before you get your job, the written communications a potential employer sees will be your résumé and perhaps an e-mail. Make sure you ask someone who is a good writer to review your writing before you send it out. At your school, there are staff members at the Career Resource (or Career Services or Career Development) office who can help you craft your résumé.

As you respond to job descriptions and send your résumé, tailor the wording for each one. Change the "Summary" section (or whatever you call the first section of the résumé below your name) to include words and phrases that you read in the job description for the particular job you are applying for. This will make your résumé stand out. The goal at that point is to get the appointment for an interview.

While you're at the interview, if it is appropriate, ask the interviewer for their business card. (That way, you will have the correct spelling of their name, title, and e-mail address.) If it is not appropriate to ask for a business card, ask the person who set up the interview for each interviewer's correct spelling of the same—their name, title, and e-mail address.

After the interview, *within 24 hours*, send a brief note to each interviewer. We used to send these by regular mail, handwritten on a notecard, which some interviewers still prefer. But today's business etiquette allows you to send this note as an e-mail. (However, if you know the interviewer receives tons of e-mails per day, yours may get "lost" in the mix. In this case, it's a great idea to mail a note on a gender-appropriate [non-cutesy] notecard.) Whichever manner you choose, the note should include:

- A "thank you" for the person's time.
- A "thank you" or acknowledgment of the opportunity.
- Your interest in the position.

This should be a brief, concise note; it shouldn't be long or rambling. Write a few samples ahead of time and ask someone who is over 35 to read it and give you their opinion. Then you'll have something ready to write within 24 hours of your interview.

After you get your first job, your personal brand will still be reflected in your business writing. Your e-mails, PowerPoint presentations, spreadsheets, etc. will highlight something about your brand. If writing and spelling isn't your thing, find a few people who can review your writing before it goes to others. If the company you eventually work for offers various types of seminars to employees as part of its education budget, find out if there is a business writing or business communications seminar you can take to help you with that aspect of your brand.

Spoken Communications

Similar to written communications, when you're speaking in the workplace, what you say and how you say it says a lot about your personal brand.

How you speak to your friends vs. how you speak to your co-workers and boss can be (and, in many cases, *should be*) different.

Using "young slang" is a bad idea in the workplace. Saying "like" too much, stammering, and saying "um" too much makes you sound as if you don't belong with the grownups.

If speaking in a business tone isn't natural for you, you've got to practice it until it feels natural. Check to see if your school offers workshops for speaking skills. Or join a local Toastmasters club where you can practice public speaking with a safe group. (See Toastmasters.org for more information and to look up a local chapter.)

Even before you get your first post collegiate job, during an interview, you'll also want to keep your speech as business-like as possible in order to establish a good personal brand in-person. I've read and heard about many younger adults making statements during their interviews that got them crossed off the list for the job. Below are a few examples of actual phrases people in their early 20s have said during interviews. *Consider these to be the "Don'ts."* (Some students reading an early draft of this book thought these examples were outlandish and rare.

However, through my research, I found that many people in their early 20s say things similar to this. It wasn't all that outlandish after all.) Following the quote in italics are my comments in regular font.

> Interviewer: *You've been in this area for a short time. What brought you to the area?*
> Interviewee: *Well, my husband was transferred here for his job. He works for XYZ Company. They're hunting for Sasquatch professionally.*
> Interviewer: *(Pauses for two seconds, then bursts out laughing.)*
> My Comments: Never say something outlandish in an interview, even if it's true. All this woman had to say was, "My husband was transferred here." If the interviewer asked her what her husband does for a living, she could keep it simple and say something like, "He's a research scientist." Truly, mentioning a search for Big Foot ruined the interview for her.

> Interviewer: *What was your favorite part about working retail?*
> Interviewee: *Uh, lack of responsibility. You never felt like you're responsible for things. It's not like running a corporation. It's like just kind of–be like a little minion and don't take the blame.*
> Interviewer: *For the position we're looking to hire for right now, there might be a little responsibility.* (Interviewer pauses; holds out his hand toward the interviewee.)
> Interviewee: (Sips his soda.) *Sounds great to me.*
> My Comments: Are you kidding me? This is one of the stereotypes of your age group–that you enjoy positions that don't require any responsibility or "taking of the blame". If you *don't* really want the job, tell the interviewer that your favorite part of a previous job you had was not having any responsibility. Actually, even in any retail positions you held as a teenager, you had *some* responsibility.

You were responsible to acknowledge customers, making them feel welcome at the business. You were responsible to help customers select their purchases, whether you worked at a clothing store, stocked items at a grocery store, worked at a fast food chain ("...*and would you like fries with that?*"), or worked at the local hardware store. You were responsible to handle payment transactions correctly.

When an interviewer asks you what you liked about a previous job that's listed on your résumé, tell them you liked having the responsibility for _____ (*fill in the blank*). The "blank" could be helping customers make a purchasing decision (plus helping customers buy a little more product or upgrade to better quality), helping customers or co-workers solve problems, or working with the team. I'm being rather generic here so that whatever jobs you've held in the past, you can fit your situation into this sentence and come up with what to say when you are asked that question–"*What did you like about that job?*"

Interviewer: *Everybody who has come in for an interview today has pretty much explained those same things to me. So, can you describe something about you, such as a word that might describe you, that we might not have heard today?*
Interviewee: *Loud.* (Then laughs.)
My Comments: While it's okay to smile during your interview, it's usually not a good idea to try to be funny. The interviewer might not find your sense of humor all that amusing. If you are asked to describe yourself in a word or a phrase, make sure you choose adjectives that are positive and work-oriented. Look up some positive words in the chapter titled "Figure Out How Others See You: Will It Help You or Not?" Be ready to describe yourself well, coming up with phrases that the interviewer might not have heard before from the other interviewees.

Interviewer: *What would you say is your greatest weakness?*
Interviewee: *I'm like so nice and giving that I would, like, do anything for a guy–I'll just give him anything and everything he wants.*
Interviewer: *Anything?*
Interviewee: (Laughs a little.) *Yes.*
My Comments: Oh, brother. When an interviewer asks *what is your greatest weakness,* he or she means "in the context of the workplace." The standard reply should be in terms of "caring too much" about a project, in that you sacrifice your free time to get something done well and on time. Another way you can answer that question is to take something that is a strength, pull a weakness out of it, and then end with the strength again. For example, let's say you have an engineer's mind, in that you are very detail-oriented and want to work on something until it's 100% perfect before it's done. The "weakness" part of that can be that, when working with a team where the others are satisfied with something being 90% correct (when it goes to the boss, a committee, or to customers), it can cause conflict when you're the only team member who wants it to be 100% correct. Then keep talking, mentioning that those situations are good learning experiences for the team to determine when it's okay when something is 90% correct and when 90% correct is unacceptable–each situation can be different. Talking about your "weakness" in those terms shows the interviewer that you find ways to grow through this supposed "weakness." Also, by choosing a weakness that is work-oriented and not so bad, you show good judgment during the interview and that you realize who you are speaking to at that moment.

Interviewer: *Tell me about an accomplishment you're proud of.*
Interviewee: *Getting a job and sticking to it. I've been known*

to get jobs and within, like, six or seven months just be done with it.

My Comments: *<Sigh!>*. That's not a weakness to mention during an interview. If you are asked about an accomplishment you're proud of, you can mention leadership roles you took during college, a sports accomplishment, or an award you won. Mention something positive. It doesn't need to be related to a previous job. As you get older and go to interviews in your 30s, 40s, and 50s, then you will want to choose something work-related to answer this question. But when you're 21 or 22, you can choose other projects and awards to talk about.

As one more example of a poor verbal personal brand, I read a story about a 32 year old woman who was transferred to another area of her company. She had done very well in her previous position. In her new job, she was given an important client account–this was a highly visible position for her to shine.

She sat in a cubicle area where co-workers could often hear each others' phone calls. One of her first calls with the high-profile client went something like this:

Yeah, hi Carol. I'm Laurie Smith, the new account manager at XYZ Corporation, and I'm, like, psyched about working with you and developing some awesome marketing campaigns. ….and about what happened with your other vendor, like, that was a bogus situation. We won't let that happen here. That was a bummer.

Do you see what is wrong with what she said? If you do, you'll have an easier time with the verbal part of your personal brand. If you don't see what is wrong, then you've got some work to do.

Again, speaking with the types of words and phrases in that quotation are okay when you're with your friends. They're not okay in the workplace.

Just so that you're "with me" on this, I'll tell you which words should be eliminated and how that conversation can be rephrased to make her brand more business-like.

The words in that conversation that should be eliminated are the slang words. Again, using the word "like" too much makes you sound really young. Besides "like," other words that should have not been used are: "yeah, hi," "psyched," "awesome," "bogus," and "bummer."

Here is an attempt to rephrase what she said:

Hi Carol. I'm Laurie Smith, the new account manager at XYZ Corporation. I wanted to call to introduce myself. I'm looking forward to working with you and developing effective marketing campaigns.

….Yes, I heard about what happened at your other vendor. We'll make sure that isn't repeated here. I want to assure you that we'll work with you through every aspect of the campaign. If you ever have any questions, comments, or concerns, feel free to contact me right away.

Do you see the difference in these two communications? In the second rewritten version, Laurie doesn't use any slang words or phrases. She sounds professional without sounding like an old lady. She addresses the client's concerns and makes herself available to resolve issues.

Those are great ingredients for building a strong verbal personal brand!

As I was writing this, younger friends of mine gave me other slang words and phrases that are currently used by people who are between 18 and 30 years old. Some of those words sounded foul to most baby boomers who weren't familiar with the slang (even if they didn't mean anything offensive in the context of the phrase). I decided to not list them in the book because these phrases and their meanings change so quickly that it could seem dated by the time you read it. However, as you read this paragraph you might have thought of words or phrases that fit this category perfectly.

(You know who you are!) If any slang words or phrases came to your mind as you read, those are exactly the types of words and phrases I mean! Don't use them during an interview or when you're around workplace people. Saying them out loud will brand you as a young, foul-mouthed person who doesn't have enough wisdom to know when *not to use* certain words and phrases.

In a final word about speech, who can you think of who has a great *speaking personal brand*? What is it that makes their speech great for their brand? What ideas can you gain from these people and adopt as your own?

Your Ideas & Projects

In my Branding coaching program, I have clients go through their past projects and ideas, which likely had titles. They review these titles (and any catchphrases connected to their projects) to see if rewording them would be better for their personal brand, reflecting the brand they want for themselves.

At this point in your life ("pre-career"), you probably don't have much experience in the workplace in this area. Keep it in mind, though, when you get your first job. If you have the opportunity to label or name your ideas and projects, stick to words and phrases that fit your personal brand. (You'll really understand what I mean the first time one of your co-workers wants to label a project with a goofy title or phrase. If your name will be associated with the project, get him or her away from the goofiness. Better yet, have them read this chapter!)

Your Voice

You might resist doing an exercise I recommend, but it's very helpful to get your voice to reflect your brand with a good sound.

Using a recording device, record your voice and play it back. (Read something out loud. Also, you can ask a friend if you can record a conversation with him or her.)

How does your voice sound? Rate your voice on resonance, pitch, and volume.

What do you think you need to work on with your voice? Do you say, "Um" a lot? Do you use local "street" language or colloquialisms often? Do you use double-negatives? (Example: "I don't want no apples today.") Do you have a strong local accent?

There are various ways to get help with your voice. You can purchase CDs and other audio versions of "speech classes" that will help you with diction. You can find a local speech teacher or speech coach who works with adults (such as actors) who will train you and your voice. There are exercises to strengthen your volume, to help you enunciate better, and to reduce local accents. Better yet, there might be graduate students in the communications department (or speech pathology department, if you have one) at your school who can help you.

For U.S.-based English, check DialectAccentSpecialists.com for recordings for voice improvement or accent reduction.

More About Your Interview

For now, focusing on the "verbal you" for your interview is very important.

People in advertising who write for TV commercials spend a lot of time working on the beginning and ending of the commercials. They want to make sure they get the response they want from their audience.

Likewise, you need to spend some time working on the beginning and ending of what you're going to say in your interview.

Consider the following topic areas that might come up during an interview (in addition to what you're read so far in this chapter). Also, you might want to steer some of the conversation when you're answering the interviewer's questions to make sure you bring up certain points:

- Showing that you've researched the company well
- Highlighting a few of your career goals (at least for your 20s)
- Noting any accomplishments, such as work you've done on an internship, leadership goals, athletic goals, or project goals attained
- What you like about the company
- Why you want to work there
- Include some of the other topics you've read in this chapter. For example: for your previous jobs–what you liked; an accurate way to describe yourself; your greatest weakness; an accomplishment you're proud of.
- What else can you think of for this list?

For all of the bullet points above:

- What do you want to say about each item in the list?
- For each, how can you *start it* during the conversation?
- Think of a brief way to *end* each one.

Write them out–now they're notes. Then practice saying them. Keep practicing until you can say them and sound natural. You can whittle them down so that it doesn't sound like you're rambling. Also, you'll want to know them so well that you can say them without looking at your notes.

Finally, check if your school offers interviewing workshops. Sign up and get some "live" practice in advance.

Sum It Up

☑ Besides being judged on your visual identity, people will also judge you based on your verbal identity.

☑ Your verbal identity includes your spoken and written words.

☑ You may need to separate your spoken personal brand between your friends and your professional career.

☑ Realize the manner in which many of your peers speak during their interviews and once they have their job. Learn to eliminate immature slang from your own workplace vocabulary.

☑ Analyze the sound of your voice to ensure it reflects your brand. If it doesn't, purchase voice CDs or hire a speech coach to train your speaking voice.

☑ Think about what you want to say during your interviews. Then practice saying it until it feels natural and you can easily remember what to say and how to say it.

☑ Study people who have strong verbal identities. Consider what you can adopt from their *speaking personal brands* to make it your own.

Create a Brand Statement That Encompasses Your Brand

▪ ▪ ▪ ▪ ▪ ▪ ▪ ▪ ▪ ▪ ▪

Among the name-brand products you buy, almost all of the managers behind those brands create *brand messages* that they use for a while to help sell their products.

Some of their messages are *taglines*, others are *value propositions*, and others are *brand statements*.

Taglines are very short and typically don't tell you anything about the brand. Here are two examples:

Nike: *Just do it*

McDonald's: *I'm lovin' it*

You can see that the two taglines above don't tell you anything about Nike or McDonald's, what they sell, or what you (as a customer) receive as a benefit from buying their products. It's simply a brief, catchy phrase they use in promotions.

Value propositions are statements that tell a customer what benefits they receive when they buy a company's product, and it's often benefits that the competitors don't provide. Wise product brand managers find out what has ticked off the competition's customers, and then find ways to make those customers happy. Once they know what will make the competition's customers happy with *their* product, they put the *benefit* into words (a sentence or even several sentences) to articulate that benefit, which is their product's value proposition.

In an excellent example of this online, a company that sells down comforters and pillows originally stated on their website: "Finest quality down comforters." (Really? Who decides that?) Besides being boring, it really wasn't a value proposition. Digging a little further into their text, their brand manager thought their value proposition was that they don't harm the geese or ducks when they gather the down, and they provide a service to customers who purchase pillows where they'll adjust the firmness of the pillow for one year. This second item was more of a real value proposition, but it wasn't prominently displayed anywhere for a prospective customer to see.

They changed their focus so that everyone would clearly see their "perfect pillow policy" and their "always free shipping" offer. These are both excellent value propositions for this type of company that people who are shopping for pillows and down comforters would want to know. (Their competitors probably won't refill pillows and probably don't have free shipping.)

Brand statements tell you something about the product (unless it's a really well-known brand) *and* they tell you something the customer receives from the product when they buy it. Where *value propositions* can be longer phrases about benefits, *brand statements* are usually shorter messages.

For a while, Wendy's brand statement was, "Always fresh. Never frozen. That's right." Then they came up with, "Wendy's–Quality is Our Recipe." Since they're a famous brand, their statements don't have to include the words "hamburger" or "food."

Lexus is a company that has created many interesting brand statements. For their various models, they've used the following:

- *Leaves a wake of desire and envy.*
- *Built by hand. Designed for the heart.*

- *Be the envy of everyone in traffic school.*
- *The polar opposite of roughing it.*

Again, since Lexus is a well-known brand, they didn't have to mention in their brand statements anything about a car. However, a lesser-known brand might need to include "what they're selling" in their statement.

Now we get back to you.

You're <u>not</u> going to create a tagline. You already did some work on your value proposition in chapter 4. Here, we'll pull that in to work on your *personal brand statement.*

For your personal brand statement, you will include what you do (or "what you bring to the table") and the benefit your target market receives when they hire you and work with you.

You will use your value proposition and your personal brand statement both directly and indirectly as you look for a job (and, later, as you develop your career). Directly, you will use them, when appropriate, as foundational messages about your brand when communicating with your target market. Indirectly, you will keep the messages in your mind as a reflection of your brand as you go about your work and find better career and business opportunities.

In order to pull several pieces together, you'll summarize some things you've worked on already.

First, write down, once again, who your target market includes:

_____

_____

_____

_____

_____

Regarding your target market, what do they want?
What is important to them?
What do they value? (Think about your responses in chapter 2)

_____

_____

_____

_____

_____

_____

_____

What is the best way to appeal to your target market (based on what you've figured out so far)?

_____

_____

_____

_____

_____

_____

Go back to chapter 4 (pages 35 and 36) where you wrote out ideas for your value proposition and rewrite them here:

_____

_____

_____

_____

_____

_____

Now that you know more about what your target market values and the best ways to appeal to them, do you have any more ideas about value-proposition types of benefits that your target market would want from working with you? If so, write them below:

_____

_____

_____

_____

_____

_____

_____

And, again, knowing what you know now about your target market and the type of workplace you're headed for, what do you think are some of the best ways you can communicate your value proposition to them as you look for a job, and then later, after you get your first post collegiate job?

_____

_____

_____

_____

_____

_____

_____

The "Wow" Factor

Another related business idea that I teach entrepreneurs can also be applied here. I call it the "Wow!" factor of customer service.

When you have been a customer of any business, have you ever experienced such great customer service that you found yourself saying, "Wow!"? The business's employee (or the owner) did something out-of-the-ordinary to help you, and it was really great. Due to this great service, you will probably be their customer for a long time, and you will tell a lot of people about their business.

Creating the "Wow!" factor is another way to create a positive message that engages your target market, "selling" your brand to them and making them a loyal "customer." It is, in a way, another value proposition. In businesses, some "Wow!" factors can be built into its regular way of doing business. Other "Wow!" factors are "one-off, go-the-extra-mile" types of activities.

In the product/service field, a few examples of building a regular "Wow!" factor into a business would be a dentist whose staff gives patients a hot washcloth at the end of a visit (much like Japanese restaurants do); a car wash with a customer area that is clean and offers free coffee from a clean canteen area; and a customer service department that empowers its first level staff to resolve most customer issues without bringing in a manager.

Keep in mind that "Wow!" work activities do not make the person performing those activities feel drained, like a doormat, or like a work slave. When you do those "Wow!" activities that make the "customer" say, "Wow!," it should actually feel empowering to you.

Further, when you do something that is "above and beyond" someone's expectations, your brand relationship with that person strengthens, and they become more loyal to your brand.

You can also think of your "Wow!" factor as your niche—something that you bring to the table that most others don't.

What are some things you can do while you are looking for your first post collegiate job (on your résumé, during your interviews, etc.) that could make your target market say (or think), "Wow!"?

_____

_____

_____

_____

After you get your first job, what are some things you can do to make your target market say, "Wow!"?

_____

_____

_____

_____

Create Your Personal Brand Statement

In this section, you'll work further toward writing your own personal brand statement. At the end of the chapter, you'll read about how you can use your brand statement to help your career.

As an example of how a personal brand statement can come together, I'll choose myself as an example. Many years ago, a former boss told me that I was very efficient.

Let's say I wanted to parlay *efficiency* as a brand and make it a positive brand characteristic for myself.

While building my personal brand, I would study and get as much experience as possible in several areas of business efficiency. I would devise several ways that businesses could save money by working with me to increase their efficiencies (that is *their benefit* of working with me, which is my value proposition), and then I would take that attribute of mine (which would also be my expertise) to come up with my personal brand statement.

After going through all of the thought processes and exercises to create my brand statement, I might arrive at this first draft:

> *Designing efficient business processes that result in increased profit.*

That statement says what I do with my skills and expertise, and it states the benefit of *increased profit*.

Then I would continue to work on the statement in case it needs more *sizzle*. (It might be okay as it is–it depends on *who* the target market is and what they want.)

Here are three more examples of other peoples' personal brand statements:

> *Producing accurate, timely records in compliance with accounting standards.*
>
> *Developing accurate coding that results in projects under-budget and satisfied customers.*
>
> *Accurate practice of law that results in increased business for the firm.*

When businesses create advertising for products, their goal is to write something that customers understand, that creates an emotion in people who read it, and that makes people want to know more.

The same is true for personal brand statements. You want to write something that people would understand if they heard it, it should create some type of positive emotional response, and it should make people want to know more about you.

You have a few more exercises to work through. If you'd like, you can read through them first, without writing anything down, and then come back to read them again and work on it.

You're going to look at two areas: your attributes and your skill set.

Your Attributes

Take some time to brainstorm all of the attributes about yourself you can think of. You might even do this in two or three sittings. (This can stretch from "good listener" to "high intelligence" to "Hispanic heritage" to "great analytical mind"– *anything goes* here). Talk to people who know you well and ask them to tell you about your attributes that contribute well to a business.

Below is a list of *positive* attributes to help you out. (You'll notice they are all positive as compared with the attributes listed in chapter 3):

Able to deal with pressure	Eager	Organized
Accepts responsibility	Economical	Patient
Accessible	Efficient	Positive attitude
Accomplished	Energetic	Proactive
Accountable	Enthusiastic	Professional-acting
Adaptable	Flexible	Quick mind
Ambitious	Follows through	Receptive
Analytical	Good attitude	Reliable
Assertive	Good communicator	Responsible
Balanced attitude to work/home life	Good judgment	Responsive
	Good listener	Risk-taker
Cheerful	Has common sense	Sense of humor
Committed	Helpful	Skillful
Competent	High integrity	Strategic
Competitive	Honest	Takes initiative
Cooperative	Intelligent	Team player
Creative	Knowledgeable	Thoughtful
Decisive	Knows when to say "no"	Tough
Dedicated	Loyal	Versatile
Dependable	Motivated	Visionary
Determined		

Brainstorm a list below of all of your possible attributes that could be valued in the workplace:

_____

_____

_____

_____

_____

_____

_____

After you've written an exhaustive list, go through the list and choose two or three that you believe will resonate with your target market and write them below.

1. _____

2. _____

3. _____

Now, for each of the attributes written above, brainstorm ideas for how they might resonate with your target market:

1. _____

_____

_____

2. _____

_____

_____

3. _____

_____

_____

(If you need to, set aside the above exercise for a day, and then come back to revisit it.)

If you can at this time, put a star next to one of the ideas above that you like best. If you can't decide right now, come back to it later to choose.

Your Skill Set

Your skill set is a set of skills you've developed over time. This is a combination of whatever you've developed in school and in previous jobs. (In the earlier example of myself, I developed ways to work very efficiently that save time and money. So one part of my skill set is *efficiency*.)

Brainstorm: What skill set have you developed over time? If you're not sure, ask people who know you, people who you've worked with in the past, parents, teachers, etc.

Here is a list to get you started. (For most, you can add the work "skills" after each):

Accuracy	Evaluation	Problem identification
Analytical	Expressing ideas	Problem-solving
Budgeting	Flexibility	Project management
Collaboration	Gathering information	Reasoning
Communication	Interpersonal	Reengineering processes
Computer	Investigating problems	Research
Conducting meetings	Leadership	Resolving conflict
Creativity	Listening	Selling
Decision-making	Management	Supervising others
Developing the work environment	Motivating people	Teaching
	Organization	Team player
Efficiency	Planning	Thorough
Enforcing regulations	Predicting future trends	Working independently

List all of your ideas and thoughts about your skill set below:

_____

_____

_____

_____

_____

_____

Of your list, given your chosen career field, which skill do you think would most likely be the best to highlight if you only had a minute to talk about yourself to one of your target market people? **Put a star next to it.** (Meanwhile, don't cross any off the list. Everything you listed is still part of your skill set.)

Pull It Together

In this chapter, you've:
- Rewritten your ideas for your value proposition
- Written ideas for how to get your target market to say "Wow!" about you
- Brainstormed your attributes and how they might resonate with your target market, and then chose one as the best
- Brainstormed your skill set and chose several that will probably catch the attention of your target market, and then chose one as the best

Go back to what you wrote in this chapter for each of the bullet points above.

On the next page, write some words that stand out as **attributes, skills,** and **benefits to the "customer."**

(For example, when I was in my 20s, I was an accountant. I might have written my attributes as *competent, efficient,* and *good communicator.* I might have listed my skills as *accuracy, timeliness,* and *problem-solver.* For benefit to the customer, I would have listed *save money, increase profit,* and *accurate accounts.* These are all areas that are important to the people who hire accountants.)

Attributes:
_____
_____
_____

Skills:
_____
_____
_____

Benefits to the "customer":
_____
_____
_____

Now, for each attribute and skill you wrote above, what do you "bring to the table" with that attribute or skill? For example:

- Are you creating something? Developing something?
- Are you adhering to certain codes and standards?
- In your chosen field, is accuracy more important than speed? Or is speed more important than accuracy?

_____
_____
_____
_____
_____
_____
_____
_____

Summarize what you want your target market to understand is the *benefit* to the company that hires you. What do they get? (Use the various words and phrases you've chosen so far to describe yourself in this chapter.)

_____
_____
_____
_____
_____

Based on what you've written for the previous three exercises (and using the examples of other people's personal brand statements as ideas for how these are typically worded), write out a few ideas for your own personal brand statement. (Usually, the benefit will be stated toward the end of the statement.):

1. _____

_____

2. _____

_____

3. _____

_____

4. _____

_____

Of the statements above, do any of them resonate with you? Which do you think would work well if you were able to communicate them to you target market? Is there more than one that would work?

Do you have a trusted colleague or friend with whom you can share these statements and ask for additional ideas? For example, you might want to know how you can make the statements have "more sizzle," as if they were for advertising (without being "cheesy"). Generate more ideas and tweak each one to see if you can make them sizzle a little more. Keep in mind the words and phrases that will draw in your target market.

If you come up with more than one, that's okay. You might be able to use more than one personal brand statement, depending on a situation, who you are talking to, etc.

You might be able to work your personal brand statement into your résumé. It depends on your career field. For some, writing it into the summary section toward the top of the résumé might be appropriate. For other career fields, it might be better to not include it on your résumé, but to keep it in your mind (during your interview) as you communicate "what you bring to the table" and the benefits a company receives when they hire you.

Since you've already done the work in this book, starting with the details and then working toward a personal brand statement, those *details* are what you can discuss in an interview when, for example, you've communicated your personal brand statement and the interviewer asks you to elaborate. The details about your attributes and skill set fill that in and will help you to answer his or her questions.

Keep your personal brand statement (or "statements") handy. Write them and post them where you will see them. Get them stamped ("branded") on your mind. Be ready to talk about yourself and sell yourself at every moment. You never know when you're going to meet someone who can help you get your first job.

After you get that first job, continue to hone your personal brand statement. Come back to this book and reread it. Tweak your personal brand statement for your new skill set that you gain over time. Keep your personal brand statement in the forefront of your mind. You never know from where your next great opportunity will come.

Sum It Up

☑ In regard to your brand's value proposition, decide how you can communicate it well to your target market.

☑ Consider how you can bring the "Wow!" factor into the manner in which you will work at your first post collegiate job.

☑ Complete all of the exercises that go into helping you create a personal brand statement.

☑ Narrow down your personal brand statement to one (or a few) that will help you get your first job.

✔ Keep your personal brand statement handy and get it "branded" onto your mind.

✔ Tweak your personal brand statement throughout your career to reflect new attributes, skills, and benefits to a hiring company that you gain over time.

How You Can Get Known By Your Target Market "Customers"

What is the first thing that comes to your mind as you read each of the following?

- Car
- Gym shoes
- Jacket
- Hamburger

While some of you might have thought, "I want to get a car. My shoes are worn out. My jacket's too small. I'm hungry," others of you pictured in your mind a particular kind of car, gym shoes, jacket, and hamburger. Many of you thought of a particular *brand* in each category.

It works for other products, too. When I think of ketchup, I think of Heinz. When I think of tissues, I think of Kleenex. And when I think of oatmeal, I think of Quaker.

How does that happen?

The people who work at those companies work very hard to ensure that when we think of a product in their category, *we think of their brand first.* This is called "creating *top of mind* awareness" in *my* mind (when I'm the consumer).

Once I, as the consumer, make a particular brand "top of mind" in my mind, I automatically assume that the brand is superior to others in the category. The brand *may be* superior or it may be no better than their competitors' brands. The point is that I, *the consumer, target-market person,* **think** it's superior. And that's all that matters to the product brand manager.

When I think of *their brand first,* I will buy it. And I might tell other people about it.

Just as visibility makes a product brand "top of mind," so does visibility make you (your *self-brand*) "top of mind" in the minds of your target market.

In this chapter, you will develop a *visibility plan* that will help you get known by your target market "customers." This is something that you will continue to do throughout your career—you'll work at getting known and visible by other target market people so that they think of you first when there are new job possibilities and projects that need a great employee to fill.

In fact, developing a visibility plan is a lot easier to do once you have your first job! Before getting that job, you'll need to get creative in order to get visible.

Keep in mind that if people think you want to get to know them only because you want something, they're probably not going to help you. Take time getting to know people and they'll be more than happy to help you. Show interest in a lot of people listed in this chapter. That way you won't just be putting forth yourself, but you'll be getting to know the other person as well. People like to know that a relationship is a two-way street.

Your Professors

A colleague of mine mentioned that she suggested to her daughter (a sophomore) that she talk more often to a particular professor in order to look toward getting an internship.

Her daughter responded, "Mom. Dr. Smith doesn't handle internships at my school."

Her mother said, "Do you realize that the professors know each other, talk to each other, and socialize? Dr. Smith knows many teachers on that campus, several of whom *do* arrange and manage student internships. If you show interest and initiative in being a hardworking future employee, Dr. Smith might highly recommend you for an excellent internship opportunity when he's talking with a key professor."

It's true. Your professors are a terrific resource for your future career. Many of them will have connections to people in several career fields. Some will have connections through their writing, speaking, and consulting work.

Show interest in other types of work your professors perform (besides creating tests for you to take). Show interest in your field, in the opportunities that are out there for you, and demonstrate that you are a hard worker.

If someone from the corporate world comes to one of your professors in a year or two and says, "Who do you think would be a good candidate for this job opening?" (and it's in your career field), what do you want your professor to say?

If you want him or her to mention your name, that's only going to happen if you are "top of mind" in their mind. And the only way that will happen is if you've created that top-of-mind awareness in them by being visible, getting to know them, and getting into their heads that you are a hardworking, energetic go-getter who is eager to graduate and start your career.

Professors don't want to be disappointed that they recommended the wrong student for a position. Be the right person!

Find out when the professor has open office hours. Stop by to visit once in a while. Remember what you read in this section. You don't need to be a pest. Just get visible and get your *positive personal brand* into your professors' minds.

Internships

Internships are–by far–the best way to get experience, get career-related work listed on your résumé, and get known by your target market.

If you haven't done so yet, find out about the connections your school has for students to do internships in your field.

- Who arranges and manages internships?
- What companies arrange internships with students from your school?
- When do they conduct the interviews?
- Will you need a résumé? If so, who can help with that?
- When are the internships actually done? (All semester? A part of a semester? In the summer?)
- How many credits do you get for the internship? (If it's not many, will you need to take a summer school class to make up for it?)
- Is this a paid or non-paid internship? If it's paid, about how much does it pay?
- Do you know any seniors who have done (or who are about to do) an internship?

Get to know the staff at your school who arrange the internships (or who arrange the interviews for students for the internships). Find out all of the details. You want to be ready for whenever they're looking for students for great internships.

Do students in your career field usually interview with all of the companies that offer internships? Or do they just interview with a portion of them? (If you don't interview with every company, find out who decides which you will interview with for the position. If you get to choose, find out how you should choose the best for you.)

You've already read about interviews earlier in this book regarding your personal brand, and there are many other resources out there that tell you how to interview. I'm not going to repeat that here. I'm assuming by "interview time" you've worked on your personal brand to the point that you are bringing your "A" game to the interview.

Weeks before your internship interviews, get help writing your résumé. Again, your school has resources to help you write a great résumé. Make sure you get a job description from the person who arranges the interviews and internships. If the job descriptions vary from company-to-company, tailor the "Summary" or "Objective" section toward the top of your résumé to closely match the job description. That means to create a slightly different résumé for each company's interview (if their job descriptions vary). Since it's not the early 1980s any more where you're typing your résumé on a typewriter and getting it photocopied, this is easy for you. Create a separate Word document (filename = Your name + the company's name + Year-month) for each résumé for each separate company. Even if you're asked to provide an electronic copy of your résumé ahead of time, *always* bring two copies of your paper résumé to each interview!

If the internship is not going to be in the area where you go to school, will you be living at home during that time? Will you need transportation? If you don't have a car yet, you'll need to figure out your transportation plans *before* your interview. When the interviewer asks how you'll get to work, you don't want to look like a deer caught in headlights.

If you will receive only a small number of credits for the internship, you may need to take a summer school class or two in order to make up for the missed credits. I took summer school classes, one each for two summers in a row, before my junior year and before my senior year, because the internship I "planned" to get only gave students two credits. I found this out when I was a sophomore and planned for it. I got a class list from the community college near my home and worked with my school to choose two classes for which they would accept the credits. This worked out nicely and there were no bad surprises.

My school was on trimesters, and, in my field, the internship was during the winter trimester. With the credits from the two summer school classes I took, I was able to take a light, full-time load during my final spring trimester of my senior year. (*That* was really great.)

You'll need to know ahead of time whether the internships arranged through your school are paid or not. When I was in college, all internships were paid. I had not heard of "no-pay" internships at that time. I had two internships, in fact, that paid very nicely. We were paid about 5% to 10% less than a newly hired graduate. A lot of students can't afford to not be paid. Or the "no-pay" internship needs to be done during a regular semester because they need to work for pay in the summer. Find out about this ahead of time. Talk with your parents about what you can afford. If you can't afford to do a 40-hour-a-week "no-pay" internship, find out if any companies that do "no-pay" internships would be willing to have you work a part-time internship. Find out if other students have worked out creative "no-pay" internships in the past. Talk with the professor or staff person in charge of student internships to find out if any of the companies involved in "no-pay" internships are willing to negotiate the hours worked.

Speaking of other students, if you don't know anyone personally at your school who has already done an internship in your field (or who is about to do one), talk to your professors to get an introduction to an upperclassman who has completed (or who is about to complete) an internship. Once you've met him or her, ask a lot of questions. It's all fresh in their mind right now. Find out what they wish they had known when they were in your shoes.

I actually did two internships when I was in college. I found out about one on my own. The other was arranged through my school. Both were huge opportunities for me. I double-majored in accounting and business administration. The internships were both in accounting. For the internship arranged through the school, my accounting professor established many relationships with public accounting firms both near our school and in Chicago. Representatives from these companies came to our school to conduct the interviews on campus in the fall. Our internships went from the week after Thanksgiving through about the third week of February. I took an internship with an accounting firm located near my school, so I remained living in the house I rented with eight other girls for that school year. (That was weird–I got up earlier than everyone, dressed up, and went to work. When I got home, they were finishing dinner.) I also had to do some business travel during that internship. Before you think, "Oh, that's cool," I should tell you that I went to Keokuk, Iowa, to do an audit with a team. (Sorry, Keokuk, but there wasn't much going on there for a 22-year-old back then.)

In the next section I'll tell you more about the second internship I found on my own.

In the meantime, having those two experiences was really helpful in letting me know what type of business environment I wanted to work in day after day. At one company, the people were pleasant to be around. In the other, however, many people were mean and, well, back-stabbing types. Not my cup of tea.

An internship helps you to get visible to people at that company. Getting in front of these people, doing an internship, and building business relationships helps you to get known by your target market before you graduate. Many times, an internship leads to a full-time job offer after graduation. You can't beat that.

Friends of Your Family and Relatives

People you've known for years (such as your parents' friends, acquaintances, and relatives) can be a great resource when you're job hunting. Some may actually be in your target market (or they will know people who are). It's important that you get reacquainted with these people. You never know who they know.

Again, you want to be "top of mind" in their minds when they're thinking about someone in their 20s who is looking for a job in your career field.

I'd like to tell you that I did this well when I was in school. However, all I can truthfully tell you is that I was really lucky *and* that I was known for being a good student who was also responsible and dependable. (Actually, that's a good personal brand when you're 21 or 22 years old and looking for a job.)

But, really, I was lucky. Here is my story.

Regarding most of my parents' friends, I really didn't know what they did for a living. I didn't know their career fields, their titles, or the companies for which they worked.

We spent many late Christmas Eves with a family we met several years earlier. When I was a junior in college, we were sitting at their kitchen table on Christmas Eve, eating cookies and talking. The man in this family (I'll call him Bob) turned to me and said, "Glory, you're majoring in accounting, aren't you?"

I told him yes, that I was.

He said, "At the company I work for, we have an internship program for accounting majors where they work for us during the summer before their senior year. It's a paid internship, too. Would you be interested?"

Would I? Um, yes.

Somehow, without the aid of e-mail or fax, I got a résumé to him, had the interview during my spring break, and easily got the internship job for that summer.

Much later, after starting the internship, I realized I had no idea that Bob was an accountant. I also hadn't known where he worked and I didn't know that he was the boss' boss. The guy was connected!

I had never shown any interest in what Bob did for a living, what his title was, where he worked, etc. That made me realize

I knew very little about the careers of most of my parents' friends. They were an entire treasure trove of people I had known for years and I never showed any interest.

Now, granted, I was relatively quiet around adults. Still, that was no excuse.

So, do you see how I was lucky? The company where I had that internship is also where I started my first job after college. The pay was great for the time. And, jobs were very difficult to find in the early 1980s. Many of my friends (who didn't go on to grad school, law school, or med school) had a hard time finding a job in their career field and ended up taking a job that didn't require a degree (or didn't require their particular degree) for at least a couple years.

The moral of that story is: Don't do what I did.

Instead, do this:

Get to know your parents' friends, acquaintances, and relatives. Make a list (if you have to) including their names, their career fields, the company they work for, their titles, and anything else appropriate.

When your parents have a party with their friends, don't disappear. Instead of leaving the house, stick around for a little while. Talk to Mr. and Mrs. Smith, Jones, Olson, whomever. Show some interest in what they do.

Most of them will ask you how school is going. After talking for 30 seconds to a minute, ask them if you can talk to them about what they do for a living. You can start it off by saying:

- "I'm wondering if I can ask you something. I'd like to know more about what people I know do for a living. Tell me where you work again…?"
- "Have you worked there for long?…Where else have you worked?"
- "What is your field?…What type of work is involved in that?"

Depending on where the conversation goes, you can tailor the rest of your questions to find out more about what the person does, more about the company they work for, their title, etc.

They will usually allow time for you to talk more about what you think you want to do when you graduate and, maybe, what you think your career path will be through your 20s. Discuss it. Ask their opinion regarding what you're thinking about your career path.

Ask them if they think you have a good plan. Maybe they'll ask you more questions about yourself and give you some ideas you haven't considered yet. The advice they offer may be helpful and it may be not helpful. (Even if the ideas they offer sound horrible to you, keep a straight face, do a head nod, and then ask your next question to slightly change the path of the discussion.) Take notes as you get ideas.

Some of these people may have excellent connections. Others may not. You never know who will have the best ideas and the best connections. That's why you need to talk with all of them whenever you have the opportunity.

Relatives may not be able to offer you a job because, at many companies, that is frowned upon, but relatives still know other people who are not related to you who may be great connections to a possible job.

Talk to everyone you know, show interest in what they do for a living and, if they offer to keep in touch, get their business card (or whatever they want to give you, such as an e-mail address and/or a phone number) and then do that–keep in touch.

I've been told that many of you are not into e-mails or phone calls; you only text. In contrast, most of the people who can help you with a job hunt are into e-mails and phone calls (including voicemail). If they tell you to send them an e-mail, then do that. If they tell you to call them, actually call them on the phone.

Only send them a text message if they specifically tell you to text them. Otherwise, don't use it.

As technology changes, there will be new methods of communication available that some people (or all people) use. The rule of thumb is (as an astute reviewer of this book intelligently noted): *Do what they do.* Whatever method of communication used by the person who is helping you, interviewing you, or making a job connection for you, use that method.

After You Start the Job

Getting visibility is something you will do constantly throughout your career in order to get your personal brand known so that when people have a new opportunity, such as a great project or a new position, they think of you.

Here is a summary of the kinds of things you can do in the future to be known by your target market customers and to stay visible:

- Join a special project or task force at your company
- Write articles for your company newsletter or website
- Write for an industry trade journal or consumer magazine
- Lead meetings at your company
- Speak at industry conferences
- Get interviewed by the media regarding your industry
- Continue building relationships with people who can connect you to other target market people

You can be concerned about the list above later. You've got enough to do now.

Keep a checklist (either in your mind or an actual list) of the people for whom you need to get visible–so that you become *top-of-mind* in their minds.

Sum It Up

☑ *Getting visible* by your target market people will help them to think of you first when they need someone like you.

☑ Get visible to your professors by spending some time talking with them so that you communicate your positive personal brand, making you top-of-mind in their minds.

☑ Internships get you so visible that they often lead to full-time job offers for after you graduate.

☑ Your parents' friends, acquaintances, and relatives are a great source for a possible job connection. Get your personal brand into their minds as soon as possible. You want them to think of you first.

☑ After you get your first job, you'll want to continue making yourself visible to the ever-changing group of people we call your target market. Find ways to stay *top-of-mind* in their minds.

Now What?

Let's summarize the areas you've read and thought about that require some type of action:

- Define and identify who your "target market customers" are, including what they like, what they don't like, and what they're looking for in candidates and employees.
- Analyze yourself accurately, as other people see you (especially your past bosses and co-workers). Figure out what aspects of yourself "fit well" with your target market customers, what aspects you need to change, and how you will change certain aspects of yourself as part of your brand–while maintaining your authenticity.
- Honestly evaluate the strengths and weaknesses you bring to the workplace. Analyze your competition's strengths and weaknesses. Figure out how to position your strengths against your competition's weaknesses to get the job.
- Analyze your "look." Compare it to what your target market customers expect from their employees.
- Decide if anything needs to change. Take a look at your "work wardrobe" and make a plan for how you will build it.
- Analyze your verbal skills–both speaking and writing. Again, what does your target market expect? How can you meet (or even exceed) their expectations?

- Work through the creation of your own personal brand statement.

- Figure out *all* of the people you need to know (and *be known by*) in order to get referrals to as many job openings as possible. Make a plan for how you are going to *get visible* by these people so that they think of you first when someone contacts them for the names of possible job candidates.

You may have read this book quickly, making a few notes here and there. Or you might have gone through it slowly, thinking through the exercises and taking more time to complete the exercises the first time through.

If you read through it without doing the exercises, let the ideas "gel" in your mind for a few days (or a week), and then pick it up again and start the brainstorming exercises before the ideas get too far away from you.

Either way you went through the book the first time, you've probably written a few notes, highlighted some ideas, and listed things-to-do, either directly in the book or in a notebook (or both).

So now what?

Go back through all of your notes. Think through them. Get the ideas really solidified in your mind.

List your "to-do's" in the order you want to do them. Then start working on that list.

If you're a senior, hurry up, for crying out loud. Skip watching TV, playing a video game, or whatever else is not school-related. Time is of the essence. Getting through the bullet list above will get a system working for you–it all works together to help you find your first great job in your field.

If you're a junior, you're just a little ahead of the curve. Use what you've learned in this book, along with your to-do lists, to get moving in a great direction. By the time you start your senior year, and you've started the work–all the way through *getting visible* to your key people, you'll have a system in place that works *for you.*

If you're a sophomore or freshman, even better! You can work your plan more slowly, figuring it out as you go, even planning how to get the internship you want while you're still in school. Keep your notes handy so that you can come back to them whenever you want, tweak your plan, and check off the things on your to-do list when you're a junior and a senior.

You could work on your to-do lists for your personal brand with a friend. It will be better if that friend is in a different career field. (Think about it. Another student in your same career field is your competition. But if competition makes you work harder, then go for it.)

It's tough out there. Some of your fellow students want the same job you want. What I told you when I spoke at your school and the information in this book is your secret weapon. Use it wisely.

Work on all of it.

Keep this book throughout your career.

Come back to it every five years, reread it, come up with a new to-do list, and work it to tweak your personal brand. Keep *you* and *your brand* on a successful career track until you retire.

Retire?

Yes. Someday.

And, until that time, invest wisely.

About the Author

Glory Borgeson is a consultant, business coach, author, and speaker with more than 25 years of business experience. She has been studying and writing about personal branding (for both corporate employees and entrepreneurs) for several years. She realized that some people have been branding themselves for a long time without actually calling it "branding." Glory also realized that many people don't brand themselves, leaving that work to others who do it for them.

"If you don't brand yourself, someone else will; and it probably won't be the brand you want!" is Glory's personal branding motto. She recalls being a young, 20-something in the corporate world where other people worked very hard to decide (for her) what her personal brand would be.

Undaunted by their bold attempts to brand her, but still not "putting words to it" (because no one called it "personal branding" at the time), Glory continued to tweak her career path, getting trained to coach others by phone, and adding writing and speaking to the mix.

After working with career people on their personal brands, Glory realized that many college students have problems with their own personal brands, as corporate managers continue to have an increasing number of bad experiences with workers in their 20s, giving these managers the impression that younger workers are not worth hiring.

Even in tough economic times when the number of graduates looking for jobs outpaces the number of jobs available, many students continue to put forth a personal brand that is far less than stellar.

Glory speaks at college campuses to let students know what they can do to develop their personal brand so that they improve their chance to get the plum job offers first.

For more information about having Glory speak at your school, or for more information about this book, see Glory's website at **www.GloryBorgeson.com**.